The Human Biography

Laura Gutman

The Human Biography

A New methodology
at the service of self-discovery.

Illustrations of Paz Marí

Translation Corina Gutman

ISBN: 9798853621428

Laura Gutman

www.lauragutman.com.ar

This book is dedicated to my children,
Micaël, Maïara y Gaia
And my grandchildren Fiona, India, Ney y Nilo

General psychotherapy methods

During the 60's and 70's, in some major cities, like Buenos Aires and New York City, there was an explosion of new psychological therapies, many following the theories of Freud, Lacan, Klein, Winnicott and, to a lesser extent Jung. Today this trend persists somewhat adapted to modern times and surrounded by a halo of virtuosity. This phenomenon has not been replicated elsewhere; in some European regions, consulting a psychologist could be considered shameful or something that only "crazy" people do. In any event, many of us still search for help, even if we don't disclose it. In the United States "faster" methods of help have been developed, such as cognitive therapies and a whole array of "coaching systems", centered on different types of consultations geared at individuals who are looking at solving specific problems of any magnitude. We live in a time when spiritual support and search for wellbeing falls more squarely within the domain of various therapies rather than a priest's counsel: neither is better than the other. This is how different cultures organize themselves.

The search for wellbeing and the understanding of our emotional states is a legitimate need. The problem arises when the methods utilized become obsolete, even if they remain popular within the collective unconscious, as if representing a warranty of success against human suffering. In Buenos Aires, going to see a therapist is as common as going to school or to work; we "all go to therapy". In friendly conversation, as soon as we touch any subject related to emotional intimacy, we might hear the comment: "I've already seen this issue in my therapy sessions". We listen and nod in approval, but what does it mean? Nobody knows. What is it that "I've already seen"? Mystery. However, we assume that if the person "has already seen this issue in her therapy sessions", her problems will slide through the appropriate channels and will arrive at a magnificent solution. During these dialogs, we assume to be talking about the same thing, however each is free to interpret whatever they want; we assume that "going to therapy" is something good and that it is a "place" where we can find a solution to our suffering. On the other hand, if someone refuses to go —especially our life partner- we assume that we will never achieve a proper resolution. Definitely, going to therapy seems to be something positive.

Psychotherapy receives good press

It is true that clients and therapists subscribing to all kinds of theories have good intentions. Typically, it is a pleasant encounter: when you "go to therapy" nobody will mistreat you. It is not like dealing with some government bureaucracy or going to the bank. No. In general we find someone who will listen. The fact that someone is willing to listen to us is like being in heaven.

We love our therapist because he listens to us. Sometimes he says something intelligent, shares our secrets, cares for us, does not judge us, agrees with us, pats us on the back and trusts our capabilities; it is a pleasure. We never received this from either mom or dad when we were children, nor from any partner during adulthood: to accept us just the way we are and exalt our virtues. Therefore, we will pay, monetarily, whatever necessary, to continue to feel that we are OK.

Is there anything wrong with this? Nothing at all, to the contrary, wellbeing is always something positive. However, we have assumed that the concept of "therapy" is something sacred, and we seldom understand what it is supposed to be. It is important to define this issue of "going to therapy", which derives from Freud's research. Since the beginning of the 20ᵗʰ century, the field of "psychology" studied in universities is based on Freud's work. Unfortunately, on one hand there is the theory - which in Freud's time was revolutionary- but something else are individuals living today, at a time when they experience much less sexual repression than a century ago. Men and women exercise a level of independence and sexual autonomy that would have been unimaginable only a hundred years ago. We know that dreams are mirror images of our unconscious and this blessed unconscious guides the strings of our conscious being. We do not argue with this concept.

After we study psychological theories, we try to make them fit within the emotional reality of those who consult with us. Here is where there is a chasm separating hypothesis from reality.

The distorted evidence

It seldom works trying to fit a square peg into a round hole. It is most puzzling why we twist the evidence so that the "it" that theoretically should be, should fit the reality we experience. I am surprised at how much we insist on upholding the validity of a theory rather than to endeavor in perceiving with accuracy the reality we experience. In my experience, theories are organized thought patterns based on reality, not the other way around.

Those of us who consult a therapist, are often obfuscated by the psychological interpretations, which are based on debatable and often biased theories. Let us assume that a person's discomfort is explained to him as the result of having been abandoned as a child by his father; not only this is a lie, but it is also a stupid explanation. To come to such "interpretation" we have to start from the "theory" that children need a positive paternal role model and that if we did not have the paternal role model, the suffering will be anchored in that childhood event. However, as I have described in prior published books, things are much more complex. There is no doubt that suffering and different kinds of emotional abandonment during our childhood could leave a deep mark in our emotional being. What I object to, is someone identifying and verbalizing "this" to be the cause of the "suffering" or being "problematic", because it may not be the case.

Childhood: a critical period

This is the heart of the matter: human beings are mammals. **We are born of the womb of a mother.** We transit an initial and very critical period that lasts a long time (the entire childhood), during which we are entirely dependent on the **maternal care**. We are dependent on the quality of that care. If the care is nourishing, loving, affectionate, abundant, soft, permanent and generous…our basic emotional safety will be assured. It does not matter if there is one father, five fathers, no father, twenty uncles, one hundred turtles or four elephants around us. It does not matter at all. Young children need —for the purpose of our comfort and our emotional and physical health- only one mother or a mothering woman sufficiently loving and available. Nothing else; absolutely nothing else.

To experience such an amazing mothering experience, our mother would need to have a very good life. She would have required a level of happiness allowing her the ability to provide wellbeing and comfort to us children. Therefore, we are introducing another aspect: based on the culture, the historical period, the geographical area, the social environment, or the civilization in which our mother lived, it will determine whether the concept of happiness will be related to a monogamous marriage, a polygamous tribe, experiencing sexual repression or freedom, with economic prosperity, with access to nature and its cycles, or whatever. Let us be clear that we are talking about the mother's comfort, not the children's comfort. Because the mother is the only thing that matters to a young child. In fact, as little children, we can live in a palace surrounded by gold, however, if we are alone, it will feel like a prison. By contrast, if as children we find ourselves in the middle of the desert under the scorching sun, but our mother's nourishing body shelters us, we will be in paradise. Please understand, **the wellbeing of a young child depends on the loving emotional closeness of our mothers**. It does not depend at all on the environment.

Let us return to the earlier example (common in many current therapies) where the interpretation is that some individuals are suffering because of the early abandonment from their father. Obviously, our mother suffered the loss of illusion, comfort and safety. It is also highly likely that during our childhood, our mother mentioned that the cause of all problems (hers and others') was and forever will be, that man's horrible decision to leave; therefore, these children will later have problems. One day for some reason we will consult a therapist and we will assume that our principal difficulty comes from having been abandoned by our father during childhood. Here we slide into a well of interpretations based on thin air, believing to have captured the cause of all ills. Unfortunately, it does not occur to us to inquire about the abandonment, the violence, the abuse, the authoritarianism or whatever that our mother exerted during our childhood instead of sheltering and nurturing us. Our mother's violence, a mother highly valued by us once we become adults, remains invisible. There are very few therapies capable of uncovering this issue.

To listen or not to listen to the client

Why is it so difficult for the therapist to detect the mechanics of the entire picture? Because nobody taught them. At university we learn theories, however we do not observe what is truly happening to us with an unbiased gaze and without any preconceived ideas. We are shifting from bias to theory; theories are pretty; however, they do not reflect our reality. Are there any good theories in psychology? Yes, there are many. There are also many great thinkers, enlightened masters and brilliant therapists, but you have to find them. Unfortunately, I have witnessed much nonsense spouted by therapists to their clients as if it were gospel; within this relationship of projections, we assume the therapist is wise, we yield to the fascination and remain caught up in the interpretations we accept as true.

The most common error, in my opinion, is that therapists listen to what the clients say. Is this wrong? Isn't it the case that people go to the therapist to be listened to? This is the heart of the matter: we continue to repeat our deceptive discourse that has been organized since childhood based on the deceptive story of the individual who named our childhood events (typically our mother). Thus, we arrive at adulthood with an established opinion about everything, based on **our own point of view**. However, when undertaking a genuine investigation, this point of view should not be considered, because it reflects a highly biased point of view we are trying to defend. Is it worthwhile for a therapist to approach the investigation by following whatever the client is defending? No. Because we will arrive at subjective conclusions, which are always wrong. In essence, we will be unable to offer the client a more complete picture, and we will continue to observe together with the client the same things with some added interpretations based on whatever theory fits this individual. In short, we failed to bring to the surface a more comprehensive understanding of ourselves.

By listening to what the client tells us, we provide the least possible therapeutic value, because the client's account does not provide a complete panorama of his life. It seems easy to accept that we must discount what the client tells us, however, there are hardly any therapists capable of finding the true logic within the picture, while simultaneously discarding nearly everything the client is verbalizing.

How do we select a competent professional, someone who can understand, observe without bias and offer a novel point of view regarding what happens to us and at the same time ignore what we are saying? I agree, this is very difficult to do. Our best ally will be our **intuition**, that subtle interior voice that alerts us when something is true, fits our emotions, or the words that can name with certainty something we knew but were unable to tolerate before; sometimes it is the opposite, we feel that the path is elsewhere even when we do not know where. We often do not pay attention to these messages. We attend the sessions because the therapist tells us that we should not abandon the "treatment". What kind of "treatment" are we talking about? This is not like taking an antibiotic, this is a spiritual journey, it is not a treatment. As in any genuine search for meaning, we may take detours any time we think is necessary. The collective unconscious bestows on all therapies a "halo" of sacredness that plays to our disadvantage. We do not feel the right to disagree, to abandon meetings, change, find something else, select a different method or another professional. However, while undertaking a personal investigation we should always preserve and maintain our internal freedom and deep inquisitiveness; anyway, if we are wrong, nothing is lost.

How do we know if the interpretations offered by the professionals are valid? First, I do not believe in interpretations, because they tend to be subjective, tinged with the professional's thoughts and feelings of value, which seldom provide clarity or fit within each client's logic, particularly if such interpretations do not bring a global, compassionate and transparent picture of the entire scenario. Most interpretations are based on psychological theories instead of mustering the courage to delve honestly and creatively into each specific and unique setting.

Couples' therapy

What happens when two partners in a relationship want to consult together? First, I doubt the veracity of the message: "we want to do this together". In the majority of cases the women want and the men acquiesce, which is not entirely wrong. What happens is that the women take the lead in the emotional realm and are more accustomed to making alliances with the "psy" professionals; women love psychology; the issues of the heart find a more yin, soft and whispering environment where we feel comfortable. That is one reason why we consult with all manner of specialists. The men, on the other hand, we prefer environments that are more yang and concrete, such as sports, economics or systems based on logic. Regardless, the men suffer just as much, however we are not as desperate to consult about our emotional intimacies. Therefore, when the women say: "my partner and I want to schedule a consultation", it is best to let the woman take the first step and let her search until she finds what she needs for herself and leave her partner in peace.

When couples come to a consultation together, the meetings tend to be rather superficial; we use the meetings to establish sustainable agreements and to have a witness who can function as the tiebreaker. This could be very interesting but it is not a therapeutic investigation, perhaps it becomes another form of mediation; maybe there will be kinder conversations; maybe one of the partners needs a witness, otherwise she fears to confront her partner when he is actively violent or out of balance. Couples' meetings can be beneficial for a myriad of reasons, but I doubt they are useful to tackle the infantile mechanisms and the individual's shadow that pulls the strings of our behaviors within the relationship. The professional will need a lot of experience and knowledge to approach each player from the point of view of their infantile realities, and attempt dealing with the conflicts that are surfacing.

When women ask that our partner join us in a psychotherapy session, it is because we want to find a discreet solution to a systemic issue within the relationship. This cannot be achieved. Other times we drag out partner to therapy because we disagree on issues that concern us both, such as the raising of our children. The women hope that the therapist will side with them, then it will be two against one. The women win. This is an absurdity. We are asking for solutions before we are willing to observe the entirety of our fabric. Unless we fully understand how we have woven the conflict, we will be unable to unravel it.

This is true for couples' therapy as it is for individual therapy: we cannot expect that the therapy will solve our problems. At best we will get started on a path of deep questioning to help us better understand ourselves and be able to observe our life's picture with a wider lens. Then, perhaps, we will possibly find the resources we need to implement changes, and perhaps those changes could modify or soften some of our problems. This is the most honest expectation we can have from any worthwhile therapy.

Is it helpful to send children to therapy?

How do you select a good therapist specialized in children? To send a child to the therapist is to bark at the wrong tree; children are dependent on the adults; we depend on an affective, economic and familial level. If the child suffers, it is the adults raising this child the ones who need to assume there is something we are doing wrong and therefore the child is suffering terrible symptoms. No matter how many times the child goes to see the therapist, he cannot change his circumstances at home. Sending a child to therapy is like "getting rid of the problem". If a child misbehaves, disobeys, gets sick, is anxious or distracted, doesn't do well in school, suffers night terrors, has phobias, does not eat, or whatever, it means that the child is expressing, he is letting us know what he is needing. It is the adults who need help to understand him, if we are willing to observe, first and foremost with the wide lens our own infantile picture, the resources we had utilized to survive and our own disabilities when it is our turn to love our children.

In fact, first we will need to understand and have compassion for the emotionally neglected and hurt child we have been, because if we are unwilling to get in touch with those wounds that have torn our soul, we will be unable to connect to what happens to our real child today. It is impossible for us to feel our young children's suffering of until we can feel, using the emotional resources we have available now, what has remained hidden since our sorrow-filled childhood. We need to soften up, go back and connect with what happened to us; we are adults now and nothing bad is going to happen to us. However, it is our children, our pupils, our grandchildren and our friends who urgently need us to review these issues. Let's not send our children to the psychologist, there is nothing to do there, especially if the children do not want to go; they are bored, it does not fulfill anything. It is not the children who need to understand what happens to them. If the children suffer for any reason at all, it is the responsibility of the adults, and to the extent that we decide to remain ignorant about the affairs of the soul, we will be unable to understand what happens to our children. That is why, the only urgency is for the adults to begin their spiritual initiation.

The spread of psychotherapy options

Since we are not specialists in the subject, when we are faced with a multitude of psychotherapy methodologies, how do we know which one to select? It is not an easy task to find a trusted professional among so many choices. However, in principle, any method could work. The method is a tool –generally a valuable one- that facilitates the human connection between the client and the professional. As in all other human endeavors, we need to find out which tools and which professionals will be best for us; our own intuition will help us find the answer. It is important to understand that to "go to therapy" involves discovering new points of view: troubling, painful but real. The therapy needs to provide a new way of seeing ourselves; it needs to fit something inside and spur us to be more in charge of our actions. If we feel like "nothing is happening", why do we continue to pay a professional only because she says it is the right thing to do?

This issue regarding the length of the therapy is something to take into consideration. I believe that working with the same professional for many years is not very beneficial to help us face our own shadow, because the professionals are human beings and we naturally become affectionate with the clients. When this happens, we lose objectivity. I believe that the most efficient treatments are short and to the point. If the professional is a good fit, she will hit the point quickly. The information we need to discover about ourselves should not take too long to be uncovered; otherwise, "the method" is not very effective, or perhaps the professional is not sufficiently competent.

Therapies are not comfortable places, it is neither a place to return to again and again because we are not feeling well, nor because the therapist understands us. No, therapy is a moment of personal discovery; once approached, understood, revisited and trained, it should become a genuine tool of personal connection at the service of our lives.

Some people are very curious, and we jump from one therapeutic method to another, because we want to learn more and more. Multiple methodologies and points of view have been developed based on the personalities and research of different professionals and teachers offering a variety of options. If they help us towards the understanding of our own being, and we can utilize each lesson to benefit us and our fellow human beings, so much the better. It is also fair to mention that some of us love to try out the latest fashion in methodology. This does not mean that we have ever tackled the understanding of our shadow. No therapy is better or faster by itself; no one is so amazing as to resolve all our problems. The different methods are tools to be employed by a capable professional and to be honored by each one of us.

I am more confident in some methods than others. This is an issue of personal preference, and no one needs to agree with me. The family constellations created by Bert Hellinger, the sacred languages, such as astrology, tarot or numerology, bioenergy, enneagram, the reading of akashic records, Gestalt, body therapies, breathing therapies, conscious fasting and yoga… are some approaches to the soul that are often revealing because they observe the human being in its entirety.

On the other hand, regarding the Freudian-Lacanian psychology, or psychoanalysis, I must admit, I have never heard of a single person obtain a higher level of self-understanding or to be able to relate something personal with a higher degree of coherence or responsibility, nor be able to show a different point of view in the understanding of their personal situation as a result of this therapeutic experience. I am often left dumbfounded by the paucity of spirit, the prejudice, the cliches, the projections of supposed understanding, and the **abuse of power** committed by the "psy" professionals. I cannot continue to ignore or uphold the untouchable sacred cows of traditional psychology on their pedestals where we have placed them, because it is unsustainable despite our best efforts. I no longer want to be condescending just to be kind and respectful towards my colleagues, because the ravages and the confusion they exert over their clients –of whom I am witness- makes it impossible.

Unfortunately, every year there are hundreds and hundreds of young people graduating from university, who believe they can understand, support and help their fellow human beings, just because they have received a psychology degree. It brings me to despair. The general confidence we place on them is disproportionate with the experiences of those "therapeutic encounters". Throughout the years, at my conferences, psychologists have always posed the most prejudiced, and even envious, questions. Eventually I realized that they were unable to fit my proposals within the "theories" they had studied; they were trying to make them fit in their minds; by contrast, individuals with other trainings formulate questions from their hearts, from their open wounds or from their true desire to better understand and think more deeply. The "non-psychologist" individuals allow themselves first to feel with their entire being what they are hearing, and then try to define if it is helpful or not. When listening to my description of the terrible helplessness so frequent during childhood and the cruel reality experienced by most children faced with isolation and loneliness – only a psychologist is capable of asking: "Well, but what happens with the Oedipus complex?" We are talking about thousands of millions of children never seen, never caressed, never understood, never accompanied, never loved by their mothers... does anyone know how to fit that harsh reality within a supposed Oedipal complex? Who cares? Only the pride of someone who studied something and is incapable of recasting a subject he once studied, and which obviously no longer serves him at all. This is what I mean when I say that usually we want to fit the square peg of our emotional reality into the round hole of a pompous theory, instead of finding our own understanding based on our concrete, painful, physical and emotional reality.

Sometimes we don't "believe" in therapists trained in non-traditional systems, just because they do not have a "psychology degree". Without a degree, they do not inspire trust. Anyone who took all the university psychology courses, would absolutely know that the psychology degree is not a guarantee of anything. Worse yet, a medical degree is even less of a guarantee. We know that if a physician goes on to practice something other than medicine, let's say, meditation, we will give her our backing. However, if there is another professional dedicated to meditation with more experience, knowledge, wisdom, spirituality, contact and discipline, but does not have a medical degree..., we do not feel as comfortable. This is a matter of **beliefs**; although more conventional individuals we don't consider ourselves believers, we are just "pragmatic". So be it!

In our culture, university degrees are the object of excessive worship. It is curious that especially in the humanities, young adults of twenty-two or twenty-three years of age, often virgins, still living with their parents in the role of dependents, never having had the experience of confronting life events, without much real experience, we complete our studies by writing a "thesis". We consult the libraries, we read all the materials we can get our hands on, we search the internet, we "copy and paste" (literally) clicking on our computers the important phrases, trying to arrive at a sustainable concept. Then we "defend" this thesis in front of professors as uninterested as we are on the subject matter of our thesis.

We celebrate by hurling eggs and flour (at least this is an Argentine tradition) and the thesis ends up in a dark corner where all the theses are kept, which no one will ever read because they are insignificant. The thesis is not going to change anyone's life. They do not resonate. There is nothing true there. Nevertheless, the blessed and long-awaited diploma gets framed and displayed prominently in the home. Now we feel capable to work with those seeking help.

Wise therapists

On the other hand, there are many notable professionals in the field of human relationships, with twenty, thirty, or forty years or experience. Individuals who have traveled, became tangled in strange events, fell from grace, were reborn from the ashes, have mingled with human misery, abuse, death, our own or another's horror, have cried, have thought, have search for resources, offered their virtues to our fellow humans, screamed our errors to the four winds, served in just and unjust causes, have fasted, prayed, listened to unrepeatable confessions, have worked to the limits of their strength, raised children, have known love and despair, had sublime sexual experiences, aged, increased their compassion and comprehension toward our fellow human beings. Sometimes we have even believed to have had a conversation with God; every so often we know to follow his direction…, even when we do not have a diploma that will vouch for this wisdom. This is when the universities should call to grant us the diplomas earned, to certify to the communities that yes, these are wise men and women who are available to help their fellow humans. Everything else is a circus. Without experience there is no wisdom. There is only arrogance.

This happens much too often in the world of "psy" and in the world of conventional medicine. The most dangerous part, is that the young people who have just obtained their diplomas, believe we know more than our clients. This is our crime. The day we are convicted of these crimes, there won't be enough jails to hold us all. Undeterred, we continue to believe this is the natural order of things: doctors and licensed people know best. This is not the natural order; this is a lie and an abuse of authority. Lies bring only chaos, ignorance and illness.

Patriarchy in the psychotherapist's office

Here is another absurd situation that is very prevalent: therapists threaten their clients with the terrible dangers they will encounter should they leave the "treatment". What are we talking about? From my point of view, it appears to be a joke; unfortunately, it is a common practice in the therapeutic office, and no one questions it! How can the therapist determine what a person should do? Especially if the individual feels with all his being that he needs something else! We can understand why so many people do not dare act against the supreme voice of any run-of-the-mill therapist, because many come since early childhood from a history of abuse and emotional submission and are accustomed to understanding love as a place of emotional obedience. It is of utmost importance to understand that a therapist is not a wise person; she is a person just like us, trained with intellectual tools. In addition, most psychologists are not even trained in the skills needed to assist suffering people. We have read lots of books, but we have very little experience, and much less the habit of thinking independently, without repeating like a parrot what we studied. However, this halo of intellectual superiority ravages the internal freedom to act of thousands upon thousands of individuals. If a therapist tries to convince his client to continue the "treatment" against their will, although the client has expressed in every possible way that they want it to end, change, rest, try something else or what have you, we should doubt no more, we need to run away from there as fast as we can.

Other times, the opposite may happen, the therapist may "discharge" the client. This seemed very strange to me: the individual feels lost, we don't know what to do on Tuesday mornings, which we had dedicated to visit the therapist. We feel a "void" and it seems unjust that he has "abandoned" us. This shows that the therapy was not effective since any therapeutic endeavor must empower the individual with more resources than he had before. I know that we often use the therapeutic space as a "trash can" where we discharge and vomit our fury and we "feel better"; but this is not a genuine search for the dark places inside, neither brings us to a deeper understanding of ourselves. It is just a temporary and superficial relief. If we have not matured…, it is evident that we will need to continue visiting the therapist since we are missing having a mother who can receive us with affection in her home. Having a comfortable therapeutic office to go to is nice but it is not therapy.

Therapies can be positive, revealing, interesting or nefarious. Sometimes they are just a great waste of time and money. We adapt to the therapeutic relationship in the same way we do in other relationships: submissive, fearful, infantile, disconnected, arrogant, or exhausted. In fact, this relationship between client and therapist should be the beginning of a path towards maturity, conscious selection and responsibility.

Will there be a time when we are feeling truly well? The objective of an effective path to personal discovery is not wellbeing…, but the understanding of oneself. The comprehension of oneself will bring wellbeing as a result, because there is nothing more comforting than to be able to better understand oneself and our fellow humans. This is a logical consequence, not an objective in and of itself.

Methodology for constructing of the human biography

Brief history of this research and methodology

Over many years of research, I have developed the **human biography** method. It developed organically, after much listening and observing with a wide lens across hundreds of scenarios. My *leit motiv* has always been that everything happens within a logical context. People are biased observers, that is why we do not understand what happens to us; sometimes we are in total disagreement with what is happening to us. Nevertheless, what happens to us, belongs to us. Other people's opinions (in this case the therapists') are built upon our biased point of view; therefore, opinions are not trustworthy. The best role of a therapist should be that of the "devil's advocate", to observe from a contrarian or opposite, better if uncomfortable, point of view, so that the picture is "complete".

In the early 1980's I began working with new moms. I have told the story many times and it is also included in prior books: I was a young mother, exiled in Paris during the Argentine dictatorship. I always had a natural availability to connect with babies and children and raising my own was not an effort. However, I soon perceived the suffering of other mothers of young children. They were immersed in an abyss of loneliness, bitterness, craziness and depression, and more than anything, they were scared by their inability to understand their babies' universe. I had the certitude, that something seemingly evident and simple for me, was not so for everyone else; women cannot comprehend the babies' universe because we do not understand our own. To me it was obvious that the moms and their babies would share the same universe; however, the distance separating her from herself was the cause that triggered the mothers to be so incredibly, painfully distant from their own children's intimate experiences. It hurt my very bones to witness the French babies cry inconsolably in their strollers while their mothers walked unmoved, bundled up in their coats cutting through the icy Parisian air. Obviously, this does not happen only in Paris, it happens everywhere. But to me, it happened every day, walking with my children, one holding my hand and the other held against my breast, through the 14eme Arrondissement. Written like this, it almost seems glamorous, but it wasn't. I was poor, did not have sufficient warm clothes for the winter; I was very, very cold. We did not have enough money; we suffered xenophobia and rejection. Those were difficult years.

At one point I returned to Buenos Aires and devoted myself to accompany mothers. There, I offered a place to be listened to, a warm tea, some hugs, a dedicated thought and the invitation to return with their babies which became a true paradise for hundreds of isolated moms on the edge of collapse. Toward the late 1980's and early 1990's, I called them "Crianza Groups". It was an open space for mothers, their babies and young children to attend with the intention of thinking together about what was happening to them. There I was able to confirm what was obvious to me: the universes of the mothers and their babies were the same. I called this phenomenon "emotional fusion" (this is described in detail in my books *La maternidad y el encuentro con la propia sombra,* translated to: *Maternity, coming face to face with our own shadow* and Puerperios *y otras exploraciones del alma femenina.*

If the universe was the same, it did not matter that much to understand what worried us about the baby, but it was necessary to go inside our own universe. In "that universe shared between mother and child", even more, in "the unknown places within this universe", that is: those parts of ourselves we do not admit, which we call the shadow. I began my research in that direction. Much water flowed under the bridge and several years later I summoned up the courage to write books, many years later I was able to publish and after many more years those books became the indispensable reference materials for mothers everywhere.

Unfortunately, many mothers used my books as a tool to confront their partners, sisters, friends or neighbors, instead of helping them to think more deeply. I regret that at times my books have been used as "artillery" to win battles in favor of something or against something else. Many readers have missed the most engaging proposal: the opportunity of posing new questions, because our opinion will always be a biased perception of our entire reality. Our ideas are worthless, our positions have no value, we do not need to be right, we only need to explore those aspects that are still unknown because of fear, immaturity or inability to decide.

After many years of working with the "mothers", the "fathers" showed up, with their own childhoods in tow, their worlds, deceits, blindness and suffering. I dedicated myself to ask the same questions which brought up painful and forgotten scenarios. Soon I realized that the apparent reason for the parents' consultation: their children's problems, was immaterial. We hardly ever discussed the subjects that worried the parents, because when we "enlarge the lens" and investigate their own childhoods and their own emotional realities built upon those experiences…there was so much to unpack and understand, that the original issue of a misbehaved child, who could not potty train or would bite, became a minor one. On the other hand, if the mother, the father, or both, were willing to review their own scenarios…later they would be able to reach their own decisions regarding the child. They would be able to understand themselves, change, make new agreements, become more generous, stop being afraid, have a genuine emotional connection. The relationship with the children will improve because of the depth and candor with which each adult has reviewed his own personal **human biography**; that is, their own childhood; their relationships with their own parents, grandparents, uncles, neighbors, siblings, predators, saviors, abusers, deliverers, thieves of the child's soul, or those who participated in the physical and emotional fabric of our early lives. If the adults are not able to look at the entire picture, why should we discuss the child? Who am I to tell another adult what to do with his own child? How could we tell the story starting from the end? It is impossible: a story told backwards is an invented story. We are talking about our lives; to tackle them, we must start by looking them in the eye, accepting the reality; knowing that reality is paramount. Reality rules. I insist, it is of utmost importance to observe in the most comprehensive manner the weave and weft of the adult family's past; always from the point of view of the child we have been.

Unfortunately, it is much easier to ask someone else, to

whom we have delegated the role of knowledge, the question as to what to do. Even today, adult men and women ask me about specific subjects regarding their own children as if I knew anything about them. I do not know. Nobody knows. Unbelievably, they ask for "advice". What is this of asking for general advice from someone who does not know them? The magazines geared to women inflict untold damage in this regard. As if life could be resolved with tips. The "tips" have become a magical spell to resolve things. My books are very poorly ranked for this purpose because they do not propose solutions to the challenges of child-rearing. These books are an invitation to formulate new questions, to take advantage of the crisis periods that are inevitably brought upon us by the presence of the children in our lives.

My research started by working with the mothers, then I began to realize that the clues could be found in **the childhoods we had lived** and what we unconsciously decided to do with what had happened to us. We all had childhoods, men and women alike. We all suffered to a greater or lesser degree. As I was intuitively searching for ways to listen and organize concepts based on complete pictures, working as the devil's advocate, it turned out that those individuals who were most eager to understand themselves, were the ones who elicited my enthusiasm to work with them. Sometimes those individuals were mothers of children, other times they were mothers of adolescents or young adults; they were women who never had children; or they were men; sometimes men without children, or older men, grandfathers, men married for the third time, men or women of mixed families; young men or women without children and far from the idea of having them; homosexuals with or without children; artists;

foreigners; young people crazy with love; individuals wanting to understand themselves more. A little bit of everything.

From the mothers to all the women and all the men

After many years, the "mothers" ceased to be the object of my team of professionals' and my research. We no longer assist those who hold onto the idea of receiving good advice about raising their children. You won't find anything further from my universe. Even if this idea continues to exist in the collective unconscious, regardless of my efforts to explain, explain and explain that here we research the dark corners of the soul and that is our only invitation. We do not promise anything more. Our goal is not to find the solutions to everyday life. With some luck, with conscience and arduous internal work, the primary objective would be to connect with our true self and the capacity to love our neighbor, which we had lost as the result of our stolen childhoods.

For the last several years, I have trained many individuals interested in learning the tools of the **human biography**, encouraging them to work with an innovative, unbiased, creative, broad and generous gaze.

To accompany another in observing their own shadow is a complex, ungrateful and thankless task. You must have a very solid emotional structure, life experience and a great desire **to serve**. Thus, I have developed a systematic work "method". I do not like the word "method"; I am not trying to box-in our work within a classification, but I do not have a better way of conveying it. I want to transmit a certain spirit to be evoked within this work. The decision to teach

-to help develop professionals who can learn to work with freedom, selflessness and true love- has encouraged me to create a system. I need to "theorize", that is, organize thoughts based on case studies, make different "paths" available and review the outcomes each day, to refine, improve and reach a level of excellence we all deserve.

This is how I designed this therapeutic method which I call the construction of the **human biography**. I admit that what I am writing today may become obsolete in a few years' time, when I will likely write something else as this process continues to evolve.

The dilemma regarding any methodology, stems from the fact that my team of professionals are constantly assisting real people and, in each encounter supporting an individual, new questions arise, new possibilities, new approaches, new perspectives to consider, to unwind the deceived discourses so deeply rooted in us since ancient times. It is an art, it can be learned, it requires creativity, inventiveness, intuition, and a modicum of playfulness to allow us to try out, risk, propose or tear apart in our thinking process, a deeply ingrained belief system and well-established bias.

Our friend, the **human biography**, we call her affectionately by her initials: the HB. To those who work in this field we designate them as HBrs, or human biographers.

To learn this trade

How can we teach the use of this methodology if it changes all the time? That is the real challenge: we use one part of methodology mixed with many parts of intuition and connection with our own internal being. It is also essential to know that, even when we attempt to cover as much territory as possible, it will always remain just a swatch of our being. People are like icebergs, we manifest a small portion of our entirety; we are comprised of many layers, of which we can only discern a fraction. In addition, each one of us embodies our ancestors' history and, since they did not resolve their own stories, it is our responsibility to solve them. Sometime, someone must be responsible for the actions of all the characters of the past; otherwise, we are delegating to our descendants the accumulation of violence, selfishness, abuse, desperation, and craziness that will spark confusion and sow illness among future generations.

Even when it is difficult to simultaneously consider all these aspects, it is important to acknowledge that they are always present and manifested in a myriad of ways. When we observe each person's **human biography**, we must keep in mind that the aspect manifesting as the problem, such as the illness, the conflict or the suffering is submerged within something much larger. We need to observe from high above and capture its entirety, by taking into consideration the spiritual force that moves this life. It is our duty to understand the meaning of this one life and uncover its highest purpose.

We are in front of an immensity. We must understand our limitations: we will be unable to embrace its entirety, the greatness of a life holding within it the entire life of the universe; it is paramount to remember that we are dealing with only a small fraction of each person's physical, emotional and spiritual reality. Once we can organize one section, we will access another, deeper still, and on and on, in an infinite spiral of understanding.

Where should we start? A possible option is to begin

remembering the client's early childhood. The problem with this approach is that the clients will tell a story made up of deceits, as I described in detail in my books: *El poder del discurso materno* and in *Amor o dominación, Los estragos del patriarcado*. Our emotional organization, all our memories, life experiences, and interpretations of those experiences, is based on what a very important person told us. That very important person is, in most cases, our mother, because, if she raised us, she was the most important person with whom we related during childhood. Even if we remember her being cruel, drunken, ill or sadistic… at that time we depended on her, we had to defend her and organize our ideas and worldview based on the lens she gave us. We are not conscious of the degree of **emotional connection** we establish with our mothers or the person who raised us. The HBrs must identify this "emotional loyalty" to deactivate it. We need to dismantle the discourse, because what our mother told us does not coincide with our reality. Let's remember that **facts rule**; everything else is maternal interpretation. We are not interested in interpretations; we are only interested in the real facts we no longer remember.

We developed unconditional loyalty to be loved. We are faithful, consistent, fierce defenders, blind, we would give our lives for mom, for her memory, for her sainthood, and for her glory. This blindness and vital offering to our mother leaves us emptied of internal freedom. This is what "colors" our view.

Am I exaggerating? No. No one is allowed to question our mother, who, despite having had a difficult life, did everything in her power to love us. Is this true? Of course. All mothers try their best for their children; however, this is a valid point of view for the mother. We are missing the **child's point of view**, the child we have been, and who has adopted our mother's point of view as the only one valid. This is the reason why the thought patterns are misleading. We are missing what the young children, dependent on the mothers' nourishment, truly need. This ends up in the shadow. In other words, the children's basic needs: the frustrations, the loneliness, the insecurity, the unfulfilled needs, when they are not named, cannot be organized by the conscious mind. If they cannot be organized, we cannot register them, if they cannot be registered, they don't exist. Thus, there is only room for the conscious existence of our mother's discourse or point of view. When people talk about our childhood, we tell the story from our mother's point of view. **We do not have access to our own child-centered point of view.** This is precisely what we are looking for when constructing the **human biography**.

How to look for and find the point of view of the child we have been?

How do we find within the childhood memories those things we, paradoxically, do not remember? This is the challenge, and the reason why this research resembles more a **detective** investigation than a psychological "treatment". We need to find something that is not obvious to the individual; we need to reach for the shadow. We construct our own **human biography** by observing our childhood experiences from the point of view of our child's internal reality, instead of recalling those events from the point of view of the person who described them when we were children. That is an external "construction", that is valid for someone else, not for the person who is trying to understand the logic to his own suffering.

Is it always the mother who names what happens to us

when we are children? In my professional experience, this happens in ninety percent of the cases. In the remaining ten percent, the official story has been organized by an individual who has taken a predominant role in our upbringing. It could have been a grandmother, if she raised us or if we were her "favorite grandchild". In these cases, the grandmother may have waged an emotional war against our mother, where some children got stuck in the grandmother's trench while other children remained stuck in our mother's trench. Although this was not obvious to us children, the HBrs need to identify how the strategic wars were organized within the family. Depending on which was our trench-refuge, we will know what point of view organized the information. It does not matter who was right and who was wrong. If we belong to the grandmother's battalion, then everything we think and feel coincides with what our grandmother has named, including how she defined our feelings and emotions. If from the grandmother's point of view, we were intelligent and mature, we will have had no choice but to be solution-oriented, level-headed, and responsible since the beginning of times. Is it so? Partly, yes, since we were valued based on our ability to take on responsibilities. However, what gets relegated to the shadow is our need to be loved and protected as children. We already know: if we are mature, who needs protection? The grandmother, obviously. We are also aware of the details in the historical battle between mom and grandma, but we hardly remember anything about our own fears, needs, desires and fantasies because no one has verbalized them. What is illuminated on the stage will be the war of mom against grandma. Poor grandma, she suffers so much. Mom is so cruel.

There are few cases when the official story was

organized by our father. It is not very common, but sometimes we find family dynamics organized around the **paternal discourse**. For this to occur, the mother needs to validate, sustain, admire and feed the paternal story. A woman who does not admire her partner will not sustain his discourse. In general, the admiration appears because of the social, economic or cultural standing held by the man, or perhaps because of his lineage or belonging. Often this belonging is built upon a fantasy with little foundation upon reality. Nevertheless, **the points of view do not need to be based upon concrete reality**; thoughts build realities. For example, a woman admires her spouse because he comes from an educated family or multiple generations of wealth, and she adopted this identity as a foundational value. Later the mother will hold -as the official discourse to her children- the importance of family belonging or attachment to wealth, etc. The discourse comes from the father, but it is validated by the mother. Without the mother's validation, the father's discourse cannot be sustained, unless, as a rare occurrence, the mother has been declared unfit by the father and the paternal family.

The soul of a sleuth

How do we know if this is a maternal, paternal or the grandparental discourse? By investigating, there is no other way to do it. The construction of the **human biography** requires a detective's soul, a good nose, intuition, an open spirit, life experience and the genuine desire to find the truth from the point of view of the child our client has been. The HBrs need significant skill since each story has its own universe; we need to observe each life with openness and honesty to be able to connect the events with the discourse. This objective "view" requires training, but as any exercise, it can be achieved with time and practice.

What should we do after we identify who this discourse belongs to? This is a good first step, as we are much surprised that "this", which until now we have firmly believed as true, can be questioned, because it does not belong to us. It is an idea organized within a pact of faithfulness between us and our mother or her substitute. By understanding from whose point of view we are watching the events, we can dive into the possible internal, and true experiences that were never spoken.

Moving forward, we need to approach the child's true internal experience; his reality has been relegated to the shadow, because nobody has put words to it, no one was interested in it, and no one accompanied us in any of these processes. As detectives lacking trustworthy clues, we need to imagine these realities and explore them with our client. Here is where the HBrs begin to put together the picture of our childhood using the very few available puzzle pieces. If we remember in detail what happened to mom, we already have one clue: we were the ones looking at mom, rather than the other way around. This denotes a fundamental imbalance within the family dynamic; the parents must look after and be available to the children; the children should never have to support and care for the parents. When this happens —which is a recurring situation within families- we can be assured that the vital childhood processes were filled with loneliness and lack of support. Based on this evidence, we will remember the fear, the repression of our needs, the desires we never expressed and the voiceless emotional neglect in all its manifestations. This is what the HBrs will name for the first time; we will find the right words to name "this" that until now, has been relegated to the shadows: the emotional neglect. The loneliness. The fear. The responsibility we felt towards our parents. The infantile difficulties we held in secret. The shame we felt because of our inabilities. Then, we will begin to draft the first sketches of how our life evolved.

We have all experienced the gap between what we hoped to find after leaving the womb and "that" which we found. It is so common in our civilization, that it becomes the primary hypothesis of each **human biography**: the magnitude of the emotional neglect.

Has anyone been happy as a child? I am sorry to bring such bad news. It is very difficult to find a child who has had her basic need for loving fulfilled. Our civilization moves in the opposite direction; it worships the fight between the weak and the strong; we are far from being a solidary organization, what happens to most children is not that different from each other. We are more similar than we think: wealthy and poor, eastern and western, black and white, Christian and Muslim, we are all **survivors of childhood terror**.

Now, having ascertained that our childhood was much more suffered and filled with emotional neglect than we remember, we need to uncover the **mechanisms of survival** we utilized. We did something to survive despite the lack of love. These "mechanisms of survival" were deployed by a "character" who will tell the story using a plot that represents him.

The characters as mechanisms of survival

Is the "character" the same thing as our "personality"? No, it is not the same. We could be introverted (this would be our personality) and mature and responsible (this would be the role we took on, the responsible one who takes care for everyone else). We can also be introverted (personality) and be lost in the fog of our fantasies and disconnected from the reality that surrounds us (this would be our mechanism for survival, because when we float away in our fantasies, we suffer less; we are not touched by what happens to us in the present). We do not take on a "character" based on our "personality" or natural tendency, but we follow what our mother has named. This has somewhat fuzzy boundaries, because there is a modicum of our natural energy that our mother is "perceiving". For now, let us establish these general concepts and later we will look at them more specifically.

We will take on a role to be deployed in the "game" of our family dynamics; this role will enable us to deploy a certain survival mechanism and make us feel more comfortable and safer. There are many characters; it is the job of each HBr organizing the **human biography**, to detect and match the correct character with the individual, and to confirm if our hypothesis "fits" with the client's internal experience. We utilize a printed visual image for this "character"; to avoid getting lost in confusing interpretations, we use images as metaphors. In the following chapters 1 will develop a variety of concepts for the proposed images and how to utilize them.

Do individuals take on a single character or does it change? In principle, they take on only one character, within different shades. Not all warriors are the same, neither all the manipulators. There are different ways of fantasizing, of imposing our own desires, to bully, or to become sick. To better understand, later we will delve into the details by reviewing some examples.

Who figures out which is the "character" the individual has adopted during his childhood? This is the role of the HBr. It is a detective's job; to those of us with a "psy" foundation, it is difficult to learn this new approach because we have been trained to listen. However, to construct the **human biography**, we need to listen very little, or just enough. As if a murder suspect were sitting on the bench, we will ask him questions, but we cannot be blinded by the details of his answers, since without a doubt they will derail us from our goal: to find out if he is in fact the killer. I repeat, we will ask very few questions; we will listen with all our senses. On one hand we will take the answers into consideration, on the other, we will select what fits within the logic of the story, and we will ask again, or we will reaffirm the facts that appear obvious or logical. With enough training, the HBrs will point out with significant accuracy what part of their story the individual is telling from a deceived point of view without realizing it.

We have a single goal: to find the truth within the story. **We are only concerned with the truth**, and we need to discover it. The individual will be of help if we don't get lost in his deceived tales. The HBrs must put together the puzzle and confirm with the individual whether he feels represented by it or not. The individual experiences his first discovery when he can see his own emotional reality with "new eyes". The observation is clean, and the feeling of relief is enormous.

Each discovery about our childhood needs to be confirmed between the HBr and the individual; the true roles of mother, father (if there is one), siblings, grandparents, uncles, neighbors, teachers, poverty, riches, forefathers, neighborhood, culture, illnesses, belief systems, morals, lies, secrets, abuses, loves and heartbreaks.

All these dynamics must be properly described in detail, until the individual agrees it is effectively so, that his internal reality has been described with accuracy. We do not "interpret". We only look for clues, we build a hypothetic scenario, and we refine it when the individual (the "owner" of the **human biography**) agrees that the pieces fit his internal experience.

Once we have approached the individual's childhood in its true dimension -with the addition of printed images, we call the "childhood scenario"- we will already have a hypothesis about the adolescence years. The HBrs need to formulate a hypothesis before advancing into the investigation phase. We are detectives; have you ever seen a detective looking for an assassin without a single clue? It would be a waste of time. In the same fashion, an HBr cannot welcome the individual without formulating a hypothesis. We are not just going to greet him and ask: how was your week? That is not how we search for the shadow. It would be a pleasant encounter between two amazing individuals; this is wonderful, but not worth paying money for it. In this case, it would be sufficient to invite the therapist out for a cup of coffee.

Adolescence

Once we have confirmed the childhood scenario and the survival mechanisms, we will research the individual's adolescence. Adolescence is a second birth. Why do I call it a second birth? Because there is a new burst of vitality and power. During adolescence we hold inside as much strength as we deployed when we were born. We are pure fire. If the adolescents do not burst into desire -for whatever is of interest to them- it is because we have been subdued since childhood by an emotional catastrophe. If we are depressed or not brimming with energy, it is because during childhood we have suffered the repression of our true desires. Whatever happened during our childhood, during adolescence, it is manifested in all its glory. During this period, we finish consolidating our "character", our "costume" in which we will dress up to go out into the world. Adolescents need courage to cross the threshold of the home and launch themselves into "society". We will wear the same outfit we used to wear as children. When the HBrs construct the **human biography** and look at the adolescence years, we "confirm" which was the survival character that continues to be the individual's place of refuge. In the social environment, the character comes face to face with his fellow humans. If we are warriors, we will find enemies and danger everywhere; if we are withdrawn, any challenge will feel overwhelming. If we are wearing Green Arrow's costume, we will sow injuries on our path. If we are surrounded by fantasy clouds, we will disseminate around us feelings of impotence. The addicts will force those around us to nourish us forever. The princesses will assume everyone else is a subject and we will despise them. The kites will let ourselves be carried away by the wind without taking control of our own destiny.

It is very important to detect and confirm the "character", because it will tell us what "cards" the individual will play when unfolding his own scenario. It is not only a matter of how we feel or what happens to us, but also how we set up the game and how we force people in relationship to us, to play certain cards and not others. At this point a well-trained HBr knows more about the individual than he knows himself. As if the detective has already caught the assassin but is setting up a strategy to have him confess, otherwise he will not be able to demonstrate what he already knows. Please forgive me for this unfortunate comparison.

Sharing the evidence

What do the HBrs do with all this evidence? We share the sketch with the individual, if the sketch is well drafted and the pieces fit, the individual will confirm it by providing more data, anecdotes, memories that begin to pour out, clear thoughts, cries, anguish, or fuzzy images that suddenly become clear and comprehensible. We can stay in this place for a while (I don't know how long is "awhile": one meeting, five meetings, it depends on each individual), until we can confirm and "color in" the map of their childhood and adolescence. Childhood is a critical period during which children are victims of the adults' ability or inability to either love or predate them. We have no choice but to live "that" which was given to us. Adolescence is different. Even if we were very immature, we have sufficient physical and emotional strength to show our gumption, to run away, to confront our parents or to realize if we find ourselves at a dead end. We acquire some autonomy to get out of the house, to observe other situations, and acquire a different perspective, by comparing what happens in our home with other adolescents' homes. This is a fundamental tool. Even if adolescents are not yet responsible for ourselves or for what we do to save ourselves -since during this period, the adults should still be responsible for us- we can already choose a different point of view. We can look "from across the street". I have elaborated more extensively on issues pertaining to adolescence in my book: *Una civilización niñocéntrica.*

Astrology tells us that starting at 14 and until 21 years of age, Saturn (in the sky) will be "across" (at 180 degrees) the position where Saturn was at birth, that means, we are able to observe our parents, the law, and our structure of provenance with exquisite distance.

The individual will tell us many anecdotes. If we are women, we will probably have an opinion -positive or negative- about everything. If we have drawn an accurate scenario, and have identified the character that offered refuge, if we have found the image that envelops, represents and gives meaning to the individual…there is not much more that is worth listening to. To the contrary, we will arrange the cards on the table, and we will explain to our client which three or four possible alternatives are available in this game. We will describe them and ask her which one she wants to bet on. It is a very funny moment. I like it, because it shows that when we don't live in a state of consciousness, we play blindly. When we approach it like this, it is easy to play "futurology". We will provide many examples in the next chapters.

A frequent example

Let's assume that a forty-five-year-old woman blames her spouse for all her troubles, because he is not smart enough and is not doing well in his business. First, if an individual faults the other for anything, she has never looked at her own belly button. I don't even ask that she looks at her own shadow, only the belly button. It is ridiculous to blame someone else for what happens to us, because we are the ones in charge of organizing our scenario. Let us assume that we have approached this woman's childhood and adolescence; she has suffered a terrible history of emotional neglect, and to overcome the fear of her father, she has become -metaphorically speaking- a formidable boxer. This helped her develop good survival skills. A formidable boxer will typically organize scenarios of ring fights; she needs enemies to fight, and some weak partners to admire, applaud and fear her.

When she wants to have a relationship…what type of partner is she going to look for? She has two options: an enemy with whom she can permanently measure up against and maintain the spark of passion, or a weakling who admires her strength and resolve. This is what I mean when I explain that the HBr shows the cards with the evidence of the two or three possibilities on how the character - which we have already identified and confirmed- can play. The individual always responds with absolute certainty. In this example, she will say: "I searched for someone who admired me. My husband was very devoted to me, he reveled in my courage and resolve. He believed in me, he supported me, he knew I was going to achieve my goals". Probably this is what the partner did, he supported her in her goals. What the partner did not do, was not part of the plot: he did not become someone courageous, entrepreneurial or sure of himself. This was not part of the "arrangement". This was not part of the plot; therefore, it is ridiculous to ask him to change when we are not changing even one iota from the screenplay.

What would have happened if our main character had chosen the other option? If she had been in a relationship with a peer enemy, against whom she could fight on the ring? Ah… the reason for the consultation would have been different. Since the "unspoken agreement" had been for two powers to confront, possibly these encounters

47

generated some very good sex. Violence and sex, screams and passion, folly and ecstasy, fury, and fluids. When would the imbalance appear? When the sexual attraction diminished, either because of the birth of the children or because the fire is extinguishing. The reason for the woman's consultation would be the expectations that her partner be kind, soft, understanding and loving. Do you realize how ridiculous our expectations are when we look at the whole picture? However, the woman would want to consult presenting that she can't believe her husband is such a brute, and what would be an adequate solution for him to understand that he needs to treat her well, because if he does not treat her well, she will have to leave, because it is all his fault, because he is an insensitive brute.

More resources to organize the human biography

We all speak from the place of light, from where we recognize ourselves. Our opinions are screenplays written in ancient times by deceived discourses belonging to those who bequeathed us our "character". That is why it is not helpful. The least we listen to the clients, the better. It is not helpful to listen to what people say, especially when they are certain of their opinion. There is nothing to be learned. The personal point of view is always blind. In some cases, the HBr may ask what "other people say about us" (our partner, our children, parents, siblings, neighbors, employees, enemies). We will construct a **human biography** that includes the experiences, perceptions, thoughts or difficulties of other people that are in relationship with the individual we are accompanying in his personal search. Thus, we will have a more complete panorama of the individual and his way of relating. The construction of the **human biography** is important to the extent that we search for the shadow, what the person does not know about herself. To be fascinated by the tale the individual is delighted in telling us, is to be derailed from our task.

How do we detect what is and what is not important? People say a lot of things. How do we find what we really need to know? In principle, we are trying to approach the **real experiences occurred during early childhood**. Individuals organize memories based on what has been named, therefore, it is very important to remember that everything the individual is telling does not belong to him. The HBrs need to detect this with a sense of humor and demonstrate each time, how attached we are to the others' "deceived discourses." To reclaim our own genuine place is a complex task; it requires dedication and consciousness to strip away the disguise.

Do we always speak for someone else? Yes, in every case there is someone who was influential throughout our childhood who has named things according to his own lens. What was named became the foundation of our identity, regardless of what we actually experienced.

What happens with pleasant experiences? Do we remember those? Not necessarily, despite having had pleasant experiences, if they were not named, they were not transferred to our consciousness. If they do not enter our consciousness, it is as if they never existed. This is typical when it comes to the way we remember our fathers. In most cases, the mothers -owners of the discourse- have told us in detail the atrocities that our father perpetrated on us; that is why we perfectly remember the scenes in which our father complied with the perfect villain role. Not only are we unable to remember the beatings we received from mom -because she never spoke of those- but she never named dad's tenderness and patience, or the vacations with dad or that dad worked all his life to support the family. If mom never mentioned dad's tenderness, we are not going to remember it even if he was the only person who throughout our childhood held us in his arms and calmed us when we were afraid or accompanied us when going to sleep. If the pleasant experiences were not named by the owner of the discourse, they do not transfer to our consciousness, therefore, they do not have entity. One of the objectives of the **human biography** is to return its entity to each real experience. Reality is paramount. It is. If it happened, it is true. We are looking for this truth; this is what we are trying to find.

The purpose of memories

Are memories trustworthy? Memories, yes; the interpretation of those memories, no. It is important to unravel the automatic story; it seems easy, but it is not. Our memories are tinged by what was named, therefore we need patience to do the work of personal investigation, self-listening and introspection. Sometimes we need to ask the person helping us construct the **human biography** to name other events so that we can recognize ourselves in them. In our function of **detectives,** the HBrs need to pose several hypotheses until we find the right one. These are the clues we can offer until the pieces fit together. When they fit, something similar happens with the entirety of the being. The individuals no longer doubt, we feel as if our self acquires complete sense and order; it organizes itself internally as if by a magic spell.

Are there people who have not assumed any character during childhood or adolescence? Until now, I have not found any. We would need mothers who are sufficiently conscious of themselves to observe their children with clarity and accompany them with freedom and generosity in the unfolding of their own possibilities. In theory it is possible. In such cases, we would find children so well loved and supported they would not need any refuge or mechanism of survival. We need a few more generations to experience this. For now, each one has a place within the scenario, observing only a portion of their reality and only from one point of view. Fortunately, we can avail ourselves of a well-trained HBr, a guide, a master, or a sage- who can observe the entire picture from outside of the relationship field. The objective of constructing a **human biography** is to invite ourselves to observe our entire field to better understand ourselves and to make the decision to love our neighbor, even when we have not been sufficiently loved as children.

Who can become an HBr?

Who can understand this methodology of self-inquiry and become an HBr to accompany others in the construction of their own **human biography**? What are the pre-requisites? None. If we are open to first reviewing our own biography, our prejudices, our pain, our miseries, and our darkness, and are interested in this methodology, we can learn, train and then practice. I have already explained that degrees, certificates or doctorates are not important, they lack value, and do not interest me. Whomever wants to be trained, can try it. Perhaps there is one requisite, but I am not certain: it would be ideal to have

-in addition to intelligence and sensitivity- some life experience, or at least to be twenty-eight or twenty-nine years old, that is the time of the first Saturn return.

What are the primary obstacles in the construction of the **human biography**? It depends on each case. Some apprentices have the fantasy that without trustworthy memories we won't know where to start. This is an interesting challenge. If we approach it with the detective's soul, we will know that sometimes the only witness to the crime is a blood-stained handkerchief. Everything else will depend on posing many good questions, sniffing, and drawing invisible lines between seemingly unrelated facts. When there are no memories, and we detect that only one voice appears now and again…we will have to name that which the individual cannot name. This requires a good amount of perception and creativity. Just like when a child is crying, we start asking: "did you fall?", "does your tummy hurt?", "are you hungry?", "are you sleepy?", "do you want this toy?" and we depend on the child's reaction to know if we have the correct answer. In the same manner, we will name possible childhood experiences until we find the correct one. It is like a game; it is like staging. The fact that some people are unable to remember anything at all from their childhoods is an indication that the experiences were much more devastating than we suspect. Perhaps we cannot even imagine or approach with our thoughts such level of suffering. Our conscious mind "forgets" in order to protect us. This mechanism of the memory has been described in detail in my book: *Adicciones y violencias invisibles*.

One of the best protection tools people utilize, is the mechanism of forgetfulness. Why bring the painful memories back to consciousness if forgetting was such a good idea? Because one thing is to be a child, and another is to be an adult. When we were children, we needed to find safety by forgetting or denying what happened to us. As adults, those forgotten experiences act on their own controlling our lives, as if with puppet strings. We are "manipulated" or "moved" by something that remains hidden from our understanding. If we delegate our lives to "strings", we do not command, and our existence becomes chaotic and unmanageable. Adults have emotional, economic, and social resources that were not available to us when we were children. Now we can look in the face at the horror, the abuse, the lies, the emotional neglect, or the madness because we can do something about it.

Normalizing violence

What do we find most frequently in the childhood histories? **Violence, abandonment and emotional abuse**. I refer to abandonment in all its forms, children do not receive physical and emotional support in the amount they need it. The abuse is more maddening. The emotional abuse happens when an infantile mother -hungry since the beginning of times- needs to nourish herself from her children. When our memories are based on all that happened to mom (because what happened to her was named constantly), the children divert their attention, preoccupation and energy toward their mother. It should be the other way around. Our mother should have changed the direction of her gaze, her attention and energy toward our infantile needs. When the children support their mothers or parents, there is infinite disorder. Nothing good comes from this foundational imbalance.

In an ideal and orderly world, the parents would support, raise, love, and help their children. The children would not support, have responsibilities nor facilitate the parents' lives. When this happens, it is disastrous, although we find it in most family histories. This is an ecological disaster; future generations will pay for the catastrophic cost. The parental emotional abuse, particularly from the mother to her children, is a true ecological calamity, because of how invisibly it operates. A mother abandons her child, we all notice. A mother seemingly preoccupied, who floods the entire emotional environment with her concerns, confuses us. We may think that her obsessions are the sign of conscious mothering; nothing is further from this. A mother who occupies with her being the entire emotional field, forces the child to her whims; this is disastrous and leaves landmines in the child's psyche for the rest of his life. The cases of emotional abuse are the most difficult to detect and deactivate. It is complex because in these cases we are mom's first and most ardent defenders, because mom suffered so much. However, the fundamental purpose of each **human biography** is to recover our childhood. The place where we deserve to be loved and valued.

A respectful bond between the individual and the HBr

How can we name what we do not remember? Could we feel attacked if someone speaks ill of our mother? First, no one speaks ill of anyone else. Of course, mom did the best she could. In addition, she carries a much more frightening **human biography** than ours. We all have our reasons; this is not the case of blaming anyone. We must look at the entire scenario to rescue the child that our client has been, because this child cannot be found on the map, he does not have his own memories, voice, or vote. Once we have a sketch of the child's field, we will be able to name with plain words what we see. Some training is needed; it is not interpretation or judgement; it is a description of the child's true emotional states. Let's remember that what we will name -describing the true emotional state of the individual when he was a child- will never be as hard, difficult or distressing as what he endured during his childhood. Nobody will feel bad if we name things as they are. The discomfort happened already. Nothing we say could hurt more than the emotional neglect he has already suffered.

Is there a way to be truly careful with the individual? Of course, there is. We should place our humanity and compassion at the service of the person who is consulting with us. Sometimes it happens and sometimes it doesn't: the individual can "touch" something magical, the **human connection** between the human biographer and the client. A breeze of compassion, openness, understanding and spiritual opening allows the methodology we are utilizing to act concretely and within a defined format, where each individual feels at home. A responsible professional takes us by the hand toward our own darkness. It is not comfortable, but we are certain to be at the right place. The words are exact and confirming. The memories and internal feelings agree. This can be painful but at the same time we feel relief and peace.

On the other hand, what hurts are the interpretations of the "psy" professionals. Unfortunately, I have witnessed thousands of cases in which the individuals remain prisoners of debatable assertions. They hold on to the therapist's deceived discourses as if their own, which are nothing more than opinions based on their own biases or personal points of view. Sometimes, during the construction

of the **human biography**, it is harder to unravel those interpretations than to undo the deceived maternal discourse.

If the person has a specific problem, is it worthwhile to review the entire biography? Of course, there is never a specific problem, or better said, there aren't any problems disconnected from the entirety of our scenario. It is true that we all want to ask a question and leave the consultation with a solution in hand; but this is a fantasy. As if we were going to the movies, and we think that by watching the last five minutes of the film we can understand the whole plot. Sounds silly and unreliable, right? However, this is what we do with the understanding of our difficulties, sooner or later we will have to be responsible for our actions.

What happens with all the information about us that appears along the construction of the **human biography**? Can it hurt us?

This "new" information is part of the process of personal knowledge. If we thought, we had a perfect childhood and we discover the degree of emotional abandonment we endured – despite that our mother drilled into us devotion and concern for her- we will be able to understand ourselves a little bit more. We may suspect that the childhood abandonment may be related to our current adult fears, our impatience when things don't go as expected, or our difficulty in taking care of our young children. We can see the degree of our lack and fears by understanding the child who lives inside of us; and from this emotional reality, we can access the resources we have available to improve our adult life from our true emotional reality, not from the ideal or the fantasy we have created.

Many individuals are tired of suffering, they no longer have the strength to revise one more time that which hurt us in the past. However, that which hurts so much **has already happened**. Nothing can hurt more than the mistreatment, the abandonment or the abuse we experienced as children. It cannot be worse to remember, organize, understand, and recover in love; to the contrary, it typically brings relief and compassion.

To accompany an individual in the search for his shadow is an art; it requires interest, love, service and generosity, and a quick and insightful mind. We yearn to find something no one has seen; we cannot fall asleep with worn-out theories nor repeat what we have learned in prior cases; each **human biography** is a new challenge and as such, it is unique. An artist cannot paint two identical canvases, a detective won't find two identical crimes. The same happens when we take on **human biographies**.

A fundamental approach to childhood

An individual's childhood and adolescence and his unconscious election of a character to survive the heartbreak, establishes the basic terrain where he will spend the rest of his life. Therefore, it is very important to understand with clarity and intelligence the foundation on which the rest of the future structure will be supported. It is impossible to construct a beautiful building if the steel skeleton and piers are not perfectly aligned, even if the supporting structure will remain invisible inside the walls. When a building is poorly constructed, the plaster cracks, the roof and the pipes break; there is no option but to - painfully- open the walls, tear, break and cut to reveal the interior. If we only patch the surface, sooner or later the cracks will reappear. A well-constructed building can be remodeled, changed and modified without worry; we have the freedom to act because the foundation is solid.

Similarly with the **human biography**: once we have established a true and logical order in each scenario's design, we can easily figure out what options we have had. Of course, we will continue inquiring and approaching all that happened to us chronologically. In general, it is unnecessary to obtain too many details. In the detective's words: if we have found the criminal, we have proof of the crime and the case has been solved, the details will confirm the events but will not substantially change the investigation.

As we continue to "piece" together the **human biography**, to complete our puzzle, it is important to understand how the individual was able to connect emotionally with others. These relationships provide an indication of how much emotional intimacy we can tolerate. These relationships allow us to play out our character more openly. For example: if we seek refuge in depression, we will likely partner up with an action driven person. The more we complain about our partner's demands, the more we will affirm our desire to remain in our refuge-character of passivity and inertia. If our client adopts the "bullet-train" character traveling at dizzying speeds, flinging the wounded on its path, he will continue to cling to his refuge-character of never stopping despite his children manifesting increasingly severe symptoms and recurring illnesses.

This is the reason why it is important to confirm the character in action within the intimate emotional relationships. Not for the purpose of listening to the complaints about her partner, parents, children or siblings, but to confirm how she moves the pieces within her own scenario.

In some **human biographies** we need to follow the money trail, in some the sexuality trail, in others we need to follow the thread of lies and family secrets and in some, we follow the thread of false religious, moral or sexual repression. Nearly every time we will investigate how each individual portrayed his vocation or personal attributes, sometimes as desires, sometimes as demands.

When an adolescent does not express desire, attraction or vocation for anything at all, this is not the natural order of things. It means that someone took away his energy. I am sorry if I am repetitive, almost always it is the mother who robbed him of his original vitality. This reality will coincide with his character; perhaps he became submissive, without his own desire, without strength or vitality, without interests and not rooted in life. Here we can formulate a hypothesis; in such a case, the individual needs to understand that **the mother** took away what is most precious, his own vital energy and it is urgent to recover it. Now, the individual has complete freedom to do as he pleases with this new information; we have shown him the true and complete panorama; he will decide what to do with what he can now see; we do not suggest or provide an opinion on what he should do.

In some **human biographies** we find the individual had a clear vocation in the past which he was not able to develop, either because his parents did not allow, because of an adverse financial situation or because it did not fit with the family's requirements. Some individuals permanently forget this flow of genuine passion to avoid suffering; in these cases, the memories reappear during the construction of the **human biography**. When the truth finds its own place, the desires belonging to those times resurface anew. This is a time for joy, to be in touch with something pure and beautiful like the encounter with a first love. Later the individual will decide what to do with this reunion; sometimes she opens a door that coincides with many other seemingly unrelated doors she opened before.

Sexual Life

During the construction of the **human biography**, it is essential to approach the individual's sexual life starting with childhood and adolescence, discussing the likely lack of maternal body. Nearly all share this same emptiness; our mothers have not touched us; they have not hugged us sufficiently neither have they protected us with her warm body; this is where our sexuality begins to unfold or be repressed. The girls freeze and the boys disconnect the body from the mind; thus, we grow removed from our bodily sensations, carrying much ignorance and inexperience on our shoulders. It isn't hard to imagine how we approached our genital sexual lives by looking at our degree of repression, authoritarianism and emotional ignorance: some of us holding onto our inner cold, others with more sexual passion but disconnected from our hearts.

What the client relates about her sexual life during the construction of the **human biography**, can be misleading, unless we collate this information with the rest of the pieces on the scenario and we make sure they fit with real events. Our sexual lives are one way we manifest our reality; it must fit, otherwise what the individual is telling us is just a tale. Men lie more about their sexual prowess because it is more socially accepted, women also lie a bit, not so much in the social environment but within the relationship with our partner. Our sexual life is not easy, mostly because our relationships have not been easy, therefore what happens in bed will confirm our suspicions when we drafted the lines between the characters and their circumstances.

Do we always need to approach the individual's sexual life within the **human biography**? Yes, always. First, because sexuality is already relegated to the shadow, after centuries of darkness and repression, even after the proclaimed and apparent current "sexual liberation", this is an aspect of our lives that remains hidden. Our sexuality is a faithful mirror of our power, desires and love; therefore, it is the perfect guide in the search for our internal truths.

Except in some rare occasions, individuals don't talk spontaneously about our sexuality during therapy, unless the reason for the consultation is related to some specific sexual disfunction. As good investigators, we want to explore especially what the individual does not consider important.

When we enter the reality of the sexual experiences, we obtain some very valuable information for the **human biography**. In the case of women, the repressive education and authoritarianism has wreaked havoc. I am stunned by the number of young women devoid of desire, even traversing the experience of maternity without joy or pleasure, without orgasms or intimate encounters with their sexual partners, a true genocide of the feminine power. We also present this so that each woman can make her own decision regarding the aspects of her being that had been stolen from her.

Each human biography is unique

We have seen that each **human biography** has a thread, a plot, a script based on a certain logic, some are underscored by emotional abandonment, others by violence, some with poverty, the culture of work, emotional ignorance, or postwar sequels; in any case there is a scenario to observe, organize and describe within a map or an image. Each life has a chronological order (in the emotional realm, dates are of little importance; for actual events, when time is divided in days, months, seasons and years, it helps us to organize our minds). Later we will arrive at the individual in the present time.

Most often, when we chronologically arrive at the present time, those issues the individuals had such urgency in resolving during the first consultation, have faded away. Sometimes because what was unveiled is much more complex, significant and profound than the trivial and fleeting original issue. Other times, we are observing the entirety of our scenario from multiple different points of view, and therefore we are already doing something different in our daily lives; perhaps relating more openly and understandingly with our partner, children, parents or anyone who belongs to our emotional environment; we are already in a process of change, or at least we are exercising a profound introspection. This is revolutionary in and of itself, even if we are not yet fully conscious. When we arrive at this place with a holistic view of our emotional reality, we are no longer asking for solutions or alliances, we do not ask the HBr what to do because we know we are the owners of our own understanding. If we do not like the results of what we have done, we can change and do something different.

It is wonderful to reach a place where we can observe our entire field as if we were watching a movie together, eating some popcorn. You can see everything; it is so easy, so evident, so clear, so obvious. How can it be that we never saw it before? Because we were inside the play, now we have been invited to observe from outside the field; like the announcers in a soccer match, they can see the entire field from their booth; the players cannot see the entire field, they only have a partial view. When we enter the booth and we observe the flow of our lives with all the actors and actresses that have participated, we are surrounded by a feeling of compassion toward ourselves and those who participated. It is impossible to deny the perfection of each play, even if some have wounded us personally, however it no longer matters, because we can see how the cards were arranged and how we guided the game since time immemorial. We can see everything; we can understand everything.

Sometimes we look at our scenarios and even if there are some aspects we dislike, if we were to change the game…we would forego some significant benefits. In other words, often, the individuals prefer not to change anything! Is it possible? Of course, but didn't we come to the consultation because we had some problems? Yes, but we would like to solve these problems without changing the game. When we evaluate the effort, movements that we would need to make to benefit others, the change of paradigm, and being in touch with the needs of our neighbor…, we conclude that we are not doing so poorly.

In these cases, the HBrs find ourselves in a somewhat ungrateful situation, because many individuals are comfortable exactly where they are and thus, they decide not to change anything; they have the right to do so. In such cases the professionals feel miserable because we know the children are paying the price: abandoned children, children that are responsible for their parents, children who are tired of being sick, children with all kinds of symptoms.

We understand that the children are trapped and depend on whether the parents initiate or not a movement in their favor. The parents looked at their past and present scenarios and decided to continue without changing anything. What can we do from our place as HBrs? Little or nothing; at most we can review the adult's complete emotional field and vehemently and clearly demonstrate that the children are left in a place of emotional abandonment that foretells an unjust future. We can offer our availability when the individual may wish to review his plot again.

It is difficult to change when we are not the ones suffering; when the suffering belongs to others, we seldom try to modify our deeply rooted defense mechanisms, even when it affects our own children. The HBrs and the spiritual guides can bear witness and name what we see; the decision as to what to do with that belongs to the individual; it is neither good nor bad.

Altruism

Altruism is a crucial subject; this virtue refers to providing more for the other's needs than for our own. When we say it like this, it seems easy, but the inability to reach an altruistic state is the great drama of our times.

Maternity and paternity are altruistic functions, everything is in the child's favor, nothing is in the parents' favor. It is a healthy relationship; the parents offer everything to the child in exchange for nothing. During the babies' and toddlers' child rearing periods we witness the enormous difficulties adults encounter in displaying our altruism; the mothers complain that we don't have any time for ourselves, the men complain that we don't receive sufficient care from our woman. We both agree that the child is too demanding, and should be satisfied with less, therefore we will do whatever is necessary to make the child understand that he will be frustrated, he will be subject to the limits we impose and will accept the world as a hostile place and perhaps he will feel better when he grows up.

The function of "maternity" and "paternity" uncovers our disabilities. If we don't have young children, we can hide our lack of altruism since there aren't other situations requiring such level of emotional demand. In the face of our children's needs, this cannot be resolved with good will; all mothers and fathers are certain we want to give our children the best of everything, but in the presence of the child's real and concrete demands, we are simply unable to do so. Why? Because we are still hungry for the affection, protection and love, **we did not receive when we were children**.

When we approach the **human biographies** and we observe the entire scenarios of men or women with small children, we will know whether they have an emotional reserve to offer their children or if they did not have it or know it. Can it be learned? Yes, of course. How? First, we need to have compassion for the emotionally abandoned child we have been. If we can re-live intensely those emotions relegated to the shadow, perhaps we can understand our children and walk in their shoes. If instead we hold onto our characters of survival, we will remain protected making sure our infantile suffering does not come to light, and simultaneously we will establish a distance to separate ourselves from our children's internal experiences. We can select from these options once we understand our entire emotional reality.

The manifestations exhibited by small children provide a good thread to follow in the construction of the **human biographies**; not only because it could help solve a specific symptom, but because what they manifest is the **truth**. The interpretations and the mother or the father's deceived discourses are unimportant; **what happens to the child is true**; the pieces need to fit the reality.

When small children are not present in our immediate environment, we will find other indicators, illnesses, conflicts, losses, depressions, or emotional wars; these are also symptoms of the truth. The task of the HBrs accompanying the process of construction of the **human biography** is to organize, to show and to propose the missing pieces of the puzzle, to synthetize the concept with the help of an image, and to accompany the individual during a period, until he can collate, using concrete events, his own plot he is now observing with new eyes. This is all. Later, when the individual asks for help or support to take a step, of course, we can accompany her, but our task is not to force the change, not even to desire the change. The desire or the decision to change or modify something within the scenario or not, rests with the client.

The HBrs do not interfere in the individuals' lives

The professionals must exercise detachment, the lives of those who consult with us do not belong to us; the decisions the individuals make are not our concern; nobody needs to agree with us. We do not have to advise, suggest or promote to do anything. We show the consequences of historic events; for example: we can explain what happens when a child does not have sufficient emotional protection from the adults who are raising him; what happens when child has many demands placed on him, what happens to a child who is "abused" by his own mother, what happens to a repressed child, what happens to a child who does not have anyone close to her emotional world. These concepts are related to the wounds caused to the human being - against the laws of nature-. We will explain them, especially because the individuals need to verify the consequences of those heartbreaks in our own personal stories. It is our right to fully understand the devastating consequences of emotional abandonment and violence, and to review the causes and consequences of our histories of suffering. We hope to understand all the options we have available as adults to offer a more caring life for our most beloved. We hope to offer support so that everyone can exercise a more gentle, healthy and loving way of relating, we have not known until now. We can offer all this to those individuals who are searching for a deeper understanding and less suffering.

The benefits will present themselves -or not- in everyone's daily lives; therefore, it is not valuable to give advice nor compel anyone to do anything. We can only offer to widen the points of view, and above all, **to include the perspective of the child this individual has been**. This is the most important discovery of the experience of constructing our own **human biography**; this new perspective is a tool the individual will have at her disposal forever. Later, after acquiring multiple points of view, engaging in new ways of looking, thinking, relating and approaching different emotional worlds of our own and others', we will be able to decide how we want to live our life from here forward.

In this sense an HBr should occupy a relatively invisible role, as a facilitator, nothing more, someone who opens some doors for the individual to go through and then decide if she wants to continue this path or not. It is important to practice detachment from the individuals we accompany and respect toward this marvelous process we witness.

Finally, we should ask why some professionals dedicate ourselves to "this" and what is the sense of digging into the suffering of so many. I believe those who work in accompanying individuals in their process of search for their shadow, can do so because we trust that sooner or later the truth will be revealed; we love the truth, because it sets us free. We trust that to accompany someone in the discovery of the transcendental purpose of each life is fundamental in itself; for this reason, we enter the dark swamps of the human soul, because we trust the inexhaustible treasures that are hidden here.

The collective intelligence

When we accompany the processes of personal search, using the **human biography** method, my intention is to provide a wider glance, to contemplate more and more; we can always widen the lens to observe more complex scenarios. The only danger is that we could realize we were wrong, nothing is lost. In any case we will have to rectify ourselves once and again until we can find the logical thread that holds together the general plot.

Humanity -and human thought- has evolved because we exchange virtues, capabilities, tools, morals, customs, ideas, learnings and experiences. We resemble ants: we have a collective brain; we all take advantage of our neighbors' hits and misses. When individuals (or communities) become rigid and close ourselves up in our own ideas defending them with passion, we use "fear" as protection against the unknown. Thus, we miss the opportunity to access the infinite options available to us at each step. Throughout history, the least prosperous periods happened when we secluded ourselves within rigid ideas or situations that prohibited or were contrary to the exchange with something different.

I always place my bets on the relationship with the different, the "other", that which our culture or our identity does not allow us to discern. I love this time of internet; the internet facilitates exchange without restrictions, it is a highly democratic system, since any individual can use it; it allows us to relate among those who are different. The internet facilitates access to an enormous virtual library, to all the cultures and all the thoughts. Obviously, we cannot trust the veracity of all the information on the internet, but this is not the question; the importance is the infinite spread of possibilities of exchange and interposition of differences; this crisscrossing brings us closer to each other and allows us to look further afield.

How does this relate to the construction of the **human biography**? We must look further from what is evident, there is always something bigger, a higher rung, a whole that includes our small portion of reality. When we expand our field of vision, it is possible to observe more and better, we can attempt to access what is not available at first sight. The **human biography** is a possible "place" where to begin developing a thought: a life, a single individual's life, one among millions.

Is the life of a single person important? There is nothing more important to each of us than our own life. However, it is more interesting to think beyond our own boundaries and consider the purpose of our existence. If we remain unsettled by our fears, life will slip away without the possibility of offering our virtues to our neighbor. We could learn and study from anthropologists, historians, archeologists, philosophers, astrologers, those who examine and reflect upon the evolution of the world and the living beings beyond our neighborhood (our modern village). This "wider" understanding will offer a more realistic point of view to our restricted daily reality. We can learn about the flow of human history, the different civilizations, the challenges, and the tools we have utilized to survive and to find a transcendental purpose; all of these are necessary lessons. To know how we were born in past millennia, what our relationship to the universe was like, how we worshipped our gods, how we obtained nourishment and comfort, how we loved, how we understood the beyond, and how we utilized our earthly resources, can offer us an encouraging panorama and guide the course to our personal becoming.

Despite living in an era of virtual connection, we hold onto antiquated ideas, worse yet, mother's ideas, even if we are not conscious of it. Proposing to an individual to transit the **human biography** does not mean that she will solve how to wean her child or save her marriage, nor will it return the joy of life to a chronically depressed individual. No, that is trivial. Each **human biography** returns to the individual a wide, open, global and transcendental picture of herself. When each person has delved into an honest and deep personal inquiry, when she has the certainty that her new "knowing" is so, because it works for the common good, then we know it has been worthwhile.

Universal prosperity

Those who want to review our own **human biography** and those who wish to be trained in this methodology (or any other) must know that the objective is not just the wellbeing of one individual. The objective becomes our universal prosperity. To know oneself contributes to the growth of universal knowledge. It is a larger purpose.

If we try to "grow" or "know ourselves better", we will have to deal with our fear, because fear paralyzes us. It imprisons us in our crystal caves, in intelligent buildings with fast elevators and security monitors, but caves, nevertheless. What stops us from getting out? The fear we experience because of the atrocious emotional abandonment we experienced during our childhood. Therefore, it is so important to tackle "this" which we can't even remember. "This" which we cannot remember is the innumerable heartbreaking experiences of our childhood. A well trained HBr will be able to give voice to the child we have been. In order to make up, imagine or suppose certain events that the individual does not register, we need to have a broad knowledge of life and a treasure-trove of diverse life experiences.

How do we search for what we do not know? How do we obtain a trustful register of diverse experiences? I believe that experiencing intellectual exchanges with many diverse and disparate individuals will provide the largest source. Thus, we need to abandon our deeply held beliefs, our patterns and reasonings, at least for a while; then we will determine if they are helpful or not, if they add or hinder, if they enrich, or amuse us. To study, explore, listen, observe, read, learn the different...this will provide us with a wider perspective.

I have never traveled to Africa and only barely in Asia, that is, I only know the western world. I hope to visit those continents before departing this life, because if I am unable to reach those distant lands, I will think from a very partial lens, and therefore, too shortsighted. What will the world look like in fifty years? It is impossible to imagine. When I was a child, even an adolescent or a young adult, the internet did not exist, or at least most people did not have any understanding about it. And now, here we are, breathing virtually every day. If everything can change so much, perhaps what I am thinking, supporting and writing...in a few years or in a few generations will be obsolete? Then? It doesn't matter. Most likely it will be useful to other people, based on the thoughts expounded here, they will be able to think something better and more suitable for the wellbeing of humanity. I am not attached to my thoughts and ideas. I only propose to think more and more, without fear. Every individual who is ready to delve into his own being must become a door open to the unknown, and instead of searching for the known references, we need to be ready to fly into new, elusive places, ready to be reached.

Transpersonal interests

Each time we access a new **human biography,** it is a single life, but it is also a parallel manifestation of many lives, perhaps of the entire universe. Just like the entire map of the human body is contained within the iris of the eye, the earlobe, the palm of the hand, or the foot, in the same manner the whole of humanity is contained within each and every one of us, and the movement of the celestial bodies is contained within the whole of humanity and vice versa. It does not matter where we start. The purpose is to understand more and more and to reach transcendental meanings.

The solutions we yearn to obtain for our own lives are a small thing. Without a doubt, we have the right to better lives, to suffer less, and to experience fewer problems. Most interestingly we will discover that the more transpersonal our interest is for a deeper understanding of the events that weave our histories, the fewer problems we will encounter, or the easier it will be to unlock our conflicts. We are all born of a mother and a father; the same happened to our mother and father: they too were born of a mother and a father. If we have siblings, we have a greater degree of intertwining, and in no time at all we will assemble a colossal crisscrossing of ancestry and descendance, by just considering only the bloodlines.

If we include friendships, occasional acquaintances, teachers, enemies, neighbors, road companions, beliefs, furies, gods, deaths, losses, forefathers and their legacies, inheritances, desires, abortions and miscarriages, longings, personal and social wars, violence, illnesses, abuses, deceits, money, lands, gifts, teachings, just to name a few human endeavors…we will knit a dense weave of belonging, that vibrates, and determines how we function. We should consider all this to understand just a small portion of our being. The degree of our interweaving is much larger than we can encompass. "One" **human biography** contains all this. Let me be clear, no single **human biography** is in and of itself "one", therefore we need to widen our perspective, always more and more.

When I express it so, it may appear unattainable, everything is so immense…our entire lives will not be sufficient to accomplish our goal. We also need to go to the office, earn a living, pay taxes, send the children to school, go to the movies, have sex every so often, sleep, watch TV, and so on. Why complicate our lives so much? I don't expect that we tackle "everything" just to understand why our partner is so unsatisfied, but at least, let's keep in mind that what we observe in our daily lives is a very partial panorama, and hopefully we can expand it more and more. Once we are capable of contemplating one level, later we may be able to access another one more complex and so on.

At least, let us remember that we are not "one", but we are "with the other" and that "other" that we do not like and reject or despise…possibly has much to do with us. If we could always hold present this perspective, we would live our lives with more gratitude and we would trust that what happens to us is perfect and at the service of our destiny.

We share a collective consciousness and due to the phenomenon of fusion with one another, we can evolve. We can know more, live better, have a kinder world and generate better material and spiritual resources for our descendants. Equally, the experience of organizing our own **human biography** or being interested in this methodology, helps the individuals develop the habit of observing **complete scenarios**. This ongoing exercise leads us to read the news with a different perspective, evaluate the complaints of our relatives with a different availability, to be supportive of our friend not as an ally but as a devil's advocate, to ask for advice from those who tell us what we don't like. To expand, expand, expand the perspective. We can always widen the lens to observe entireties and therefore be understanding and compassionate with all. Let's admit it, we all have our reasons, us and the others, always.

Case study examples

The development of the **human biographies** that I will share with my readers in the following chapters are common examples; the individuals here described could be any of us; we are not exceptional, to the contrary, we present ourselves very similarly. The purpose is to bring this modality closer to the public, prioritizing intellectual honesty. I invite each one of us to consider our adulthood by being responsible for our own actions. There is nothing to advise others, to the contrary, this is a place to look together, contemplating the "whole". It is not our place - once we have observed together a specific scenario- to tell the individual what to do. At most, as we develop the plot

75

will bring forth the voices of those who suffer.

As in my prior books, the "cases" are not entirely true stories. I have changed the gender, professions, dates, number of children, geographic locations and any other reference that will facilitate anonymity. Something interesting happens; some individuals seeing themselves reflected in these stories, have written to me asking how I knew what had happened to them and why I made public such an intimate subject. It is funny, because not only I do not know these individuals, but I do not engage in cases "that someone told me about". I do not need them; we have thousands of real cases amid my professional team. If I wanted, I have sufficient examples to write one hundred books more. Some events are so common that individuals feel they have been alluded to and believe I am telling the world their private lives. Well, it is not so. It is very funny, because at times the names have coincided: for example, I make believe the name of the mother is Patricia who has two children named Manuel and Joaquin. By coincidence, a woman named Patricia with children with the same names has an identical story and she is furious trying to figure out who told me about her intimacies. I am sorry to confirm to you, my readers, that we are very similar, and we experience very similar events…even when we think our drama is the worst. I assure you that there are no real identities. I select common situations from here and there for the purpose of explaining the methodology in the clearest manner. Let's remember that when we go to the movies, we often identify with the characters, but we do not suspect that Hollywood found out about our private drama. Differences aside, the same happens with the cases I describe.

It is my hope that the case studies here examined can

be helpful to my readers to more easily access the methodology of personal inquiry I propose, to open the gates of our wounded emotional selves and to bring forth a true reunion with our core being.

A school for detectives

I am considering changing the name of my school, I think sometime soon it will be called "School for Detectives". This is what I attempt to teach: how to find the real tracks that will show the reality of the individual's past and present emotional field. In psychology, we are so used to the interpretations that this proposal, seemingly easy, is in fact exceedingly complex. What complicates the clear observation is the weight of the judgements with which we observe any situation. Because each of us, carries on our shoulders a backpack of **deceived discourses** and a fogged-up lens from our character's screenplay. In the following chapters I will develop this concept more clearly. For now, it is important to know that if we are unable to learn how to watch without including our judgement…we will never reach the truth.

The reality is the reality. Each scenario allows certain scenes that can be played, and discards others that would be impossible to play. As I have written in prior books, the professionals who accompany in these processes of personal inquiry work as detectives, not as psychologists. The detectives try to find out something that no one knows. However, the psychologists listen and then interpret based on what we have heard. Therefore, this keeps us in deceit.

Do not listen to the individual

We need to get used to listening very little of what our client says. We need to imagine the individual as if he were a murder suspect. If we ask the individual sitting on the accused's bench whether he committed the crime…what is he going to say? Of course, he will uphold his innocence. We don't need to ask the question, because we know the answer. If we are good detectives we will have some clues, some more evident than others. We will continue to search for the evidence. The stronger clues will be confirmed, and the others will be discarded.

Little by little we will organize the scene, and the clues will lead us to a traumatic event, we will need to ask fewer questions from the suspect, because the scenes will begin to manifest by themselves. I ask your forgiveness again for such a horrible comparison, since most individuals searching for spiritual support are far from committing a murder. I want to explain without a doubt that the "listening" rarely takes us to a trustworthy place. Since the discourses are mostly deceived, listening and validating what the individual is saying will only affirm that which is false.

I understand this job of investigating the emotional lives of individuals by asking few questions and organizing much requires training and a high degree of intuition. It is also necessary to have access to the knowledge of many, many circumstances of human life. It would be optimal for the HBrs to have gone through diverse personal experiences in love and heartbreak, to have been able to transcend cultural, ideological and moral frontiers, to have interacted in different environments and to be open and permeable people. Because the individuals consulting with us can be very different from us. We must be able to understand the logic of those whole scenarios even if they have nothing to do with our own idiosyncrasy and our way of life.

It is difficult to teach at a school for detectives, because the cases we have, have already been investigated, and there will always be a new situation, with hidden corners and secrets that we'll have to unravel using logic, creativity and intuition.

Case study: Denise

I will transcribe a class in the School for Detectives. An apprentice brings in a case from an individual who worries her. We will call her Denise. She is forty-five-years old, has two male children, one is twenty, and the other is eighteen years old, and she has recently separated from her life-long partner. She is mad at him and mad at life in general. Denise says she wants to better understand herself and wants to be able to forgive her ex-husband. She works as a high school volleyball coach.

We recommend a short tour along her **human biography**, searching for the quality of "mothering" she received as a girl. Let us remember that every **human biography** is based on what we experienced in life viewed from the child's point of view.

We learned that she came from an immigrant German family, both on her mother's and father's side. We searched for memories…and we find a great deal of rigidity and discipline from her mom, and contempt toward dad. Denise is the oldest of four children, however she cannot describe anything about her siblings. The mother said that she was "difficult". Here we uncover some initial considerations in our detective's "draft": How can you be "difficult" in a hostile, disciplined and rigid environment? It is very unlikely. Perhaps mother **said** she was difficult, but it does not mean it was so. To confirm, we ask Denise:

what did she do to be so "difficult"? She does not remember. She remembers mom's severe punishments; mom's gaze was sufficient to freeze her. She also remembers the atrocious fights between mom and dad. As detectives, based on this picture, we know that she could have been a somewhat restless child. A normal child. We know that all children "need to move", right?

In principle we can establish that "because she did not stay still", the mother named her "difficult". The apprentice who brought this "case" confirms and agrees. She adds that since she was a young child, Denise was sent to practice many sports. Her childhood is spent between the German school and the German club, both within two blocks from her house. Here is a sketch of the scene: the mother establishes how and where Denise is allowed to channel this energy. Not too bad. Other children often do not have an environment where to channel their vitality and end up being punished or "implode" in illnesses or bad behavior. We attempt to find additional childhood images, we only find the discipline in sports, but no glimpse of tenderness, care or affection.

We continue inquiring into her adolescence. As detectives, what do we think will happen? The approach to the opposite sex will be, at minimum, difficult. That is why we do not ask any kind of questions such as: "How many boyfriends did you have?" No. First we review our "detective's notebook", and we will tell Denise that the perspective looks desolate, cold and rugged. Still, she does not have any memories about her siblings, but she remembers well her participation in sport competitions and her loneliness despite excelling among her peers. She adds with pride that she didn't need anything other than winning her medals.

When she was twenty-four, already working as a volleyball coach, she has her first "love" encounters -if we can call them such- with another instructor of her same age. She gets pregnant almost immediately. She did not know anything about sex, did not even know she could get pregnant. Obviously, she did not know anything about the world of affections. We inquire about the quality of the relationship she had with this young man, but despite becoming her life companion during the following twenty years she can hardly tell us anything about him. What do we have here? At minimum, a frozen woman, hard, cold, distant…and pregnant.

We can draw a picture, we can also explain that we are searching for some warm, cozy, soft, protective experience…, but we can't find any. We can show her the picture of a female war general, someone with a well pressed suit, upright, stoic, rough. We are approaching a woman's life, but the energy is masculine. Perhaps the picture represents a woman in a general's suit, saluting, hardened and proud of her position.

The apprentice who brought this case for our study, mentioned that when she got pregnant, the mother told her: "Now you will have to sacrifice more". This was all. The mother's unconscious message was: Let's play a game to see who can display the most coldness. Events cannot be understood unless we are looking at the entire map. Something else happened, during the pregnancy, the young couple decided to move to the southern part of the country, to a very isolated and cold place, away from neighbors. Why? Because they had received in inheritance a small house from a great-uncle. It seems unusual if we think about it, looking at it from the outside. Any of us with a different **human biography** would conclude: "Now that we are expecting a baby, I want to be near the people who love me". However, the detectives look at the scenes using their intrinsic logic. Within this context, Denise and her new partner went looking for something "known" to feel safe: "this" known was isolation, dryness, desert, loneliness and austerity.

Here, the detectives could show Denise what were the experiences from the point of view of the baby born of her womb under these circumstances. If we innocently inquire: "How was the baby's first year?", Denise will say: "He was adorable, he ate and slept well". The detectives look at the entire scenario and we understand that a baby expecting tenderness and protection would necessarily suffer under these circumstances, finding himself with a young mother, frozen and rigid. Military salute. At this point we can share with her the image we have selected. Can you imagine this female general with a baby in arms? Truly, it does not fit.

We continue our investigation; we will observe together how the baby's softness does not fit the rigidity of a young woman trying to meet the requirements of her own **mother's discourse**.

When she gets pregnant with her second baby, they return to Buenos Aires and both Denise and her husband work as coaches at two different schools. Obviously, Denise won't have any reliable memories from her children's childhoods. In fact, she says she does not remember anything, as much as we keep asking.

All kinds of questions arise within the apprentices' group: "Did she recover the relationship with her mother?" "Did they abandon the house where they lived in the south?" "Did she get along with the father, who does not appear anywhere?" "Did she have any female friends?" "Did she have relationships with other mothers of young children?" "Did she want to have children?", etc. I want to show that sometimes our curiosity can play against us... Being a detective is not always compatible with being curious. To want to know all the details feeds our need to control but does not offer additional clues to our investigation. We need a lot of detective training to discern what type of questions are helpful and which lead us astray.

Many years go by without much happening. We explain to Denise that she comes from such a hostile environment and that she has identified with her mother figure, to the point of adopting her rigidity, discipline and coldness. And that the birth of each child has represented a valuable opportunity she has yet to capture. Those are the life moments when our destiny sends us signals from "our other side", in Denise's case, it was her tender and loving side. However, she did not consider it. Her "character" of female general did not allow it.

We continue investigating. How do we imagine the partnership and sexual life of this character? Obviously, not very warm. Our sexual life is generally untidy, chaotic, explosive, fiery and joyful. However, when confronted with these terms, Denise sought refuge in her value for discipline. We imagine she was ever more relentless with her children and her students. We tell her. The apprentice confirms that she has had problems with the school administration where she works because of the tense relationship and the mistreatment of the adolescents she trains. We do not judge whether this is good or not. We do not say who is right or wrong. We only look at the image of the female general. We imagine her codes, her reasons, her rage, her coldness and her identification.

The apprentice agreed that this image fits her perfectly. She added that the husband had abandoned her recently.

The General

She was furious, but had not shown sadness, fear, anguish or pain. Again, we look at the image together. The children are grown now, and despite questioning her about her children's lives, she can tell us very little to nothing. This is very shocking.

What do we do with all this? In first place, it is appropriate for us to feel -us, the detectives- this girl's pain that lives curled up inside the terrifying outfit of female general. Such is the fear instilled in her since early childhood that she has been unable to move a single inch from what her mother dictated. It is most important that we preserve the focus to perceive the individual in its entirety, from her past to her probable future. We look globally, then we look at the details to allow us to observe the broader picture.

I want to emphasize that if we had listened to all that Denise had to tell us, we would have been unable to access the real picture and would not have been helpful to the protagonist. Denise would have explained her reasons, and if they were well described, we would have listened with concern that which everyone understands and explains from their own point of view. However, the **human biography** is not constructed from a frame of friendship, we place ourselves in the hands of a detective, who is going to look at what the individual is unable to perceive about herself.

In Denise's case, she knew she was furious because her partner left her. Until now, this is the only thing she understands about herself. By accessing her broader life picture, she may be able to understand the price the other has to pay if he intends to have a relationship with her, by submitting to the rigidity and mandates of a relentless female general. In this case, it appears that the "other" got tired. Or found something softer somewhere else; it is understandable.

Will Denise change anything? We do not know, and it is not our concern. One thing is not better than another. Is there suffering? Yes, much. We assume that her children suffer, her husband suffers (even after leaving the marriage this man lives in a condition of intense heartbreak); in addition, we are placing on the table Denise's dark suffering. It does not matter how much she takes refuge in her female general's suit; the fear remains inside. Childhood fear; terror; panic; nightmares; darkness; death.

What happens if Denise does not like what we show her? Nothing happens. She is an adult. She could be interested in this new point of view about herself that brings her closer to her internal truth, or she may not want to touch the subject. She knows this is part of her being. She has no doubt about it.

What else do we need to do as detectives? Complete our work and go home. Without expectation that anyone will consider our work as positive, healthy or beneficial.

The seed of human suffering

To approach an individual's **human biography**, we need to start somewhere. Even if it is contrived, I always suggest starting with the birth. Let's not forget that the individual's birth is intertwined with her own mother's birth a generation before and so on.

When we review the passage of our lives and touch again the pain that arises with every breath since the beginning of memory…it is because this pain had a beginning. I believe the first imprint is found in the scene of our birth: it is very simple. To generate suffering in the human being, it is sufficient to separate the newborn's body from her mother's body.

If at birth, humans need and therefore expect to be in contact with the same comfort we experienced during nine months in our mother's womb, to find a lack of warmth, softness, the familiar heartbeat, holding arms, calming words, protecting body and nourishing milk, to the contrary, to find ourselves in an inhospitable empty crib without movement, it is simply, a terrifying experience. What are we going to do when confronted with this hostility? We have two options: The first is to do nearly nothing…to remain passive, even at risk of dying. Thus, we become passive or dominated. There are certain advantages to occupying the passive role -these advantages are less visible than the dominator's- we do not assume any responsibility about what happens to us, because it is the other's fault (the dominator).

When we are children, we are unable to consciously select; we spontaneously survive, according to what our energy, our role in the family, our personality or our "mysterious I", allows. When we are dominated, this lack of nourishment and protection often manifests itself when our mother has the absolute need to nourish herself from us, her children. In these cases, the children satisfy the mother's emotional holes, and to this extent we need to be alert and know everything that happens to her and what she needs. When this happens, nobody looks at us as children, nobody takes care of our needs, which should be the priority. The children's vitality is sucked away by the adult. The adult obtains energetic nourishment, and the children remain without emotional strength, without desire, originality and sense. We have been dominated, and at a critical time when we should be nourished to attain our peak splendor, we will live for the benefit of the adult.

The second option is to react, confront and fight to attempt to obtain what we need. What do we need to do to confront the situation? We display our aggression, vitality, strength and dominance. Can we do "that" when we are newborns? Of course... let's put together ten crying babies in one room... We could win one or two battles. In any case, if we "decided" to confront, we will take every opportunity to show our gumption.

When babies are confronted with a hostile situation, lacking the protection of the maternal "protecting" body, we will react. Either by becoming passive (dominated) or becoming aggressive (dominators). We will understand that life is a hard and adversarial place. As you can see, we are growing a warrior inside of us. We are afraid and know in our gut that we will have to fight constantly to survive. Nothing will be given to us if we do not fight to obtain what we need. We know we are alone, and we depend on our strength and our gumption to survive. Otherwise, we can become a martyr. A front-line soldier to be killed in the conflict. All wars need some cannon fodder.

Both "characters" suffer. When the little ones try to self-satisfy not to die, or when we confront the obstacles to the limits of our strength. We suffer the lack of love, the lack of softness, tenderness and solidarity. We suffer the deception, because we came into this world ready to love, but the world -represented by our mother- received us with a gust of fury and violence.

What is the sense of all this? Why would our civilization do this? Do we need suffering children? Indeed, without warriors there cannot be domination of the strong over the weak. Without warriors there is no patriarchy. We need a system that ensures continuity through successive generations. This system gets implemented from the very moment of birth. Each child separated from his mother immediately after birth, if a boy, will become a warrior, if a girl, she will bear warriors. Whether active or passive warriors.

The human creature original design

What is the problem? How does this process continue day after day? By creating an abyss between the babies -born yearning for love and with full capacity to love- and the reality of the emptiness that surrounds us. This is not culture nor conditioning. This is the **original design of the human species**: all human babies are born with an intact capacity to love, yearning to be protected, nourished and cared for, this is the only way to express of love during this period of our lives. It is devastating not being able to receive what has been natural during our life in the womb - the constancy of bodily contact, nourishment, rhythm and movement under the cadence of our mother's breath-.

Babies will do anything within their reach to obtain what we need: to be attached to our mother's body. How are we going to obtain this? Even when most of us were never successful, we have cried to the point of exhaustion, we fell ill, we had outbreaks, we suffered domestic accidents or infected our organs,

Unfortunately, even when our bodies manifested what we were unable to speak, because we were not yet verbal, our manifestations were only attended to at the physical level. Perhaps we were taken to a medical consultation, we were subject to an analysis, a needle's prick, checkups…without anyone allowing us to remain cuddled in the arms of a protecting adult. Watching this scene from the baby's point of view, is a great disillusion.

What do we do to survive?

As we grow up, things do not improve. On one hand, we have refined our survival tools. Each child will develop different resources, but there is something we all share: the certitude that the world is dangerous, and we need to be constantly alert. Certainly, we must attack first, there are predators everywhere and the emotional hunger will never end. Some children learn to be aggressive with everyone: we bite our mother's breast, we bite other children, we spit, hit, hurt. We experience the need of having to permanently defend ourselves from external aggressions, that is loneliness and emptiness. Other children use different strategies: we get sick. Our bodies get hot. We desperately ask for a caress; sometimes the caress arrives but it often ends as soon as we recover our health. The adults look at our tired bodies but cannot see our discouragement when we realize they are not ready to hold us in their arms and allow us to stay there curled-up forever.

Some children decide not to bother anyone, holding onto the secret hope that our mother will finally love us if we don't make her mad. Other children fill ourselves up with food, sugar, television, noise, toys, or audio and visual stimuli... not to feel the bleeding jab of loneliness. In other cases, the children directly anesthetize any vestige of pain, we become immune to contact, we stop feeling. We surround ourselves with an air-blanket around us, to the point of not tolerating the vicinity of people. Thus, we grow and develop distanced from our emotions to feel safe: taking refuge in the intellectual mind. We become intelligent, cynic, fast, ironic, unattached and critical youngsters.

We are trying to imagine what happened to us starting from the time we left our mother's womb... until becoming the people we are today. This is how we built our characters, the characters we will try to unravel when we organize our **human biographies**. This is what we attempt to dismantle: our mother's false interpretation of our defense mechanisms; those very mechanisms that helped us survive. This is, my dear reader, the **maternal discourse**. This is what it is all about. Not only how our mother named her own sadness, needs and yearnings, but how our mother named us. How our mother saw us, which is how we will manifest ourselves: with anger, pain, rage, complaints. Endless complaints. With illnesses or problems, we want to resolve right now. However, it is necessary to transit the experiences we have had from that place of needing to give and receive love, to understand this loneliness and this coldness that lives inside of us.

This is the only possible outcome, as the

consequence of emotional abandonment and lack of maternal bodily connection (I am not even mentioning those children who were threatened by their parents or received beatings, screams, humiliations, punishments, lies, emotional and physical abuse..., acknowledged or not, although these are the great majority of children). There will be a more active or a more passive reaction, but a reaction, nevertheless. This reaction, this response, will be equal in intensity of aggression or retraction to the impact received. Children learn very early on that no one is to be trusted. We are alone and we must defend ourselves. If there is something "appetizing" out there, it is better to "catch" it as soon as possible and eat it before another hungry child comes and steals it from us.

I want to demonstrate that this primary suffering - which is not part of the original design of "human being" but rather follows the logic of and is the result of our patriarchal society of domination- is the **seed of all the suffering that follows**. This is organized from the day we are born. If you think I am exaggerating, please visit any medical institution where women give birth and observe if there are babies attached to their mother's body, the only place where the child should be as soon as he exits her mother's belly.

This suffering gets stamped-on the day we are born, when we were placed at a physical distance from our mothers, and we impose on the baby this incredible loneliness; this had already been predetermined the day the mother was born and that was predetermined the day the grandmother was born in a continuum over many generations born within a domination dynamic. The separation of the baby's body from his mother's body is so usual, so common that appears to be "something normal" we no longer question.

When we come from multiple generations of frozen bodies, how can we know where to search for the "beginning" of the suffering? The "beginning" is manifested anew with **every child's birth**. Each little one, in sync with the original design of the human species, will demand the maternal body to experience love. It is possible to break the transgenerational chain of suffering, with just the decision to do so. With the consciousness that allows us to make "this" decision.

Boys and girls grow up sharpening their teeth. Ready to attack. Ready to defend ourselves, or at least to remain camouflaged, so that we are not seen by the predators. Distanced from our emotions or any other affective weakness. Another way of being disconnected from our own infantile emotions is to be flooded by our mother's or other adults' emotional events. Our mother has such a need to be seen, accompanied and embraced by others that we, as young children have no alternative but to fulfill this responsibility. Some children believe to have "matured" when we are fully capable of understanding what happens to mom; this is not maturity, this is called **maternal abuse**. As children, every time we look at and support our mother, worried, doing what we can so that "she" does not suffer… we are talking about maternal abuse. I will retake this subject in a later chapter and will offer some images to facilitate understanding.

For now, I want to clarify that even when we know everything about mom, supporting her, protecting her, accompanying her…we do not attain emotional maturity. Emotional maturity is obtained when we are standing in our own axis. Maturity goes hand in hand with self-understanding. In most cases, we depend on an infantile mother, because she grew up devoid of care and protection; as a result, the children experience a childhood where the child's place is missing, we are removed from our essential needs, and live in an upside-down family dynamic. Everything is backwards. While we are children and we are dependent on the adults who should be protecting us, we can't do anything to straighten this up.

Mom's soldiers

What is the relationship between maternal abuse and the warriors needed by the patriarchy? We become mom's enlisted soldiers. We shine her boots. We attend to her most infantile, dark and displaced needs. In this permanent care for mom, we are lost to ourselves, therefore, fed up, our upset and our tiredness will surface at a moment's notice when confronted by anyone else attempting to "take" any emotional sustenance from us.

Let's imagine when, years later, we give birth to a child..., clearly, we do not have an "emotional reserve" available to draw from. Here we can observe the **continuum of emotional abandonment:** children who nourish their mothers forever; when we become adults and it is our turn to raise our own children, these children are in their turn left abandoned and hungry, because the parents are busy nourishing the grandparents, and later this new generation of hungry children that will be called to satisfy us, will become the predators of the next generation and so on and so forth. The dynamics of abuse leaves entire generations in **sorrow**; during childhood, the one period in life when we should have **pure receiving**. The only possible childhood formula is to fill us with care and protection so that we can develop maturity and generosity during adulthood.

The warrior modalities are many and diverse. We will describe them throughout the book using concrete examples so that the dynamics can be very clearly understood; these dynamics are **survival mechanisms** caused by the emotional abandonment we experienced during our childhood.

The warrior is an absolutely necessary tool to establish domination. This domination cannot be perpetuated without someone enforcing it with the power of authority and superiority of some over others. To have a civilization based on conquest, we need to manufacture future warriors all the time. It is not by chance that we separate the babies from their mothers. This has a very specific purpose. It is incumbent upon us to look at our civilization, widening the zoom lens with a global historical view, instead of believing that centuries of history can be changed with a little will.

Much more than that. We need to agree on what kind of civilization we wish to have for ourselves and our descendants. It is not by chance that we separate the babies from their mothers, and it is not just a mistake; it is by design. If we all continue to contribute to maintaining the status quo, within the same system, based on biased opinions and repeating the same obsolete ideas as if they were a mantra, we won't get a chance to change our perspective.

A child warrior is always ready to kill or die. In our modern technological society, we can be lined up as blindly as soldiers from any historical period. We can build up massive armies of anesthetized soldiers, disconnected from our emotions, and become entirely dominated. If we continue to live without desire, vitality and transcendental meaning, we will follow anyone who is expressing any convincing idea. We will repeat opinions, will believe any run of the mill idea and will organize our lives around well-trodden paths, even if they do not remotely resonate with our internal being. During an elections period, we can read any newspaper from any country… and we will confirm how easy we can self-identify with any forcefully delivered speech and any promise of future wellbeing. It is the same thing, just a different magnitude.

Taking control of the truth

The fundamental objective of organizing the **human biography** is to let the **truth** come forth. For this reason, it is important to separate the grain from the chaff and to figure out what is deceived discourse and what is truth. Truth must be linked to reality and most often it coincides with the dictates of the heart.

A civilization organized based on the domination of the strong over the weak, needs to control the truth. Throughout human history, many wars have been waged between human beings to impose a certain group's way of thinking and organizing life over another. There are no limits to the heated discussions and bitter fights just for the purpose of imposing our beliefs and reasoning above everyone else's. This is a fundamental point in our thinking: we are not trying to be right. We do not care to be right. We only care to understand the nature of human behavior to accompany the individuals to better understand themselves.

As we approach the different **human biographies**, we attempt to unravel the mothers' deceived discourses and organize the twisted interpretations of those events that happened within each family; we often discount the children's ability to understand the truth behind the events. Deceits, lies and secrets are very common in most life histories. The families' chronicles are peppered with fallacies and concealments. Events are denied, hidden, covered-up, slandered, and adulterated.

Whosoever owns the information and does not share it, retains power. The most valuable asset to reach victory in war is to obtain information the adversary is lacking. The same happens within personal relationships.

Emotional fusion and truth

The best option to wield power in a domination-based civilization, is to start by controlling the children. Therefore, it is very common to assume that children should not know what is happening. Even more, it is better to keep them isolated from any kind of information. It is a well rooted custom to assume that children do not understand or there is no reason for them to know grown-ups' things. However, "grown-ups' things" are typically situations they experience every day and therefore it concerns them.

To leave someone without access to knowledge and information is the equivalent of keeping him prisoner. Because the other cannot make decisions about anything. Thus, there is a specific purpose every time someone decides that another should not find out about a something.

Often the adults assume that children cannot understand complex situations. Sometimes we think that to explain that grandpa will die soon would be to "burden them" and we "will ruin their happy childhood". This is such a deeply rooted custom seemingly based on good intentions, it is not so. If we were to understand the "emotional fusion" (described in more detail in my previously published books), we would know that children live in fusion, that is, at minimum, they breath the same emotional field as their mother. They also breathe the same emotional field as the father, siblings, and other individuals to whom they are emotionally linked. We are all interconnected, but the children have the honor of not having yet built too many obstacles to block that internal certitude that tells them what mother, father, caretaker, or the neighbor is feeling.

If the child lives inside the mother's emotional field – he lives inside the emotional field of his entire environment, but the mother is the principal field- it means that the child experiences, perceives, knows, breathes, smells, senses, and flows within this field that **is his own**. **The maternal field and the child's field are one and the same.** There is nothing the mother feels that the child does not feel. It is impossible. As if we immerse two individuals in a small pool with 100F water. Both will feel the heat. It is impossible for one of them not to feel anything. The emotional fusion is the same. The child is in the same pool as the mother and feels the same temperature as the mother.

It is imperative to understand the phenomenon of "emotional fusion" -I know, at some point this will be taught in university even if it happens when I am no longer on this physical plane-, otherwise we will be unable to understand anything at all about the mental organization of human beings.

It is ridiculous to assume that we can avoid telling the child that grandfather is dying. First, because he **already knows it**; second, because, while he knows it and we deny it, the only thing we accomplish is to inflict suffering. Because we are **distorting the truth**. We are telling the child that what is happening is not really happening. Going back to the prior example: the child feels that the water is warm, and we are telling him that the water is freezing. Not only we are setting up the deceit, but we are establishing the foundations of madness, which is just a great chasm between discourse and reality. This child will grow up believing with absolute certainty that hot water makes you cold. It is an absurdity!

The deceit has different "sizes". It starts from the "white lies" to a degree of misrepresentation that the person's psyche cannot tolerate. In such cases the only way out is "madness". I have described in detail the various degrees of psychic derangement and chaos in my book: *Que nos pasó cuando fuimos niños y qué hicimos con eso*, which stems from the separation between reality and discourse. At minimum we should know that **children are not born crazy**. To the contrary, insanity is a possible and healthy way to deal with misrepresentation and lies.

I no longer have patience to comply. Adults justify among ourselves the "exceptions" regarding certain realities that are "too complex" and we assume cannot be explained to the children because they could not understand it. This is false. A child is no less emotionally intelligent than an adult. To the contrary. Children have constructed fewer walls between ourselves and our own identity -mostly because we have had fewer years and we have not had sufficient time to distance ourselves from our own internal being, therefore we are in spontaneous contact with our emotional reality. This is the meeting place between the children's internal certitude and a plain explanation offered by the adult so that **words and reality coincide.**

Our bamboozled childhoods

Unfortunately, our childhoods are filled with deceptions. Not only those events our parents decided to hide from us, but the accumulation of partial points of view, belief systems and prejudices our parents believed in and transferred to us as the only lens through which to access understanding.

Nearly all families have navigated through multiple secrets and deceits that have cratered our intelligence, our ability to adapt and to hold a reasonable perception that coincides with the facts. If we want to confirm, by looking at the not-too-distant history of our parents and grandparents, we will find untold contradictions, since many of the official family stories do not fit the logic of reality. Unfortunately, many individuals continue to believe that our father died of a stroke at age 34 o that grandpa was such a good man, that he took care of some of the village children that according to the gossips were his illegitimate children even if nobody could verify it. Or that mom was born after six months' pregnancy and only grandma's love saved her. We need to confront with tenacity the official story, considering its contradictions and lies, because the naked reality does not hold up. We prefer to transit the road of banalities and stupid beliefs, not to leave our degree of comfort.

What is the point of continuing to believe that mom was born after six months of pregnancy? Because if in our family there is a lineage of devout, chaste, pure, moralistic, repressed, and prejudiced women. Who is going to say that the emperor has no clothes? Who is going to take the risk and doubt grandma Matilde's virginity on her wedding day? The funny thing is: who cares, especially if Grandma Matilde had a good time. However…the discourse is stronger than the truth. Because, if despite the excessively repressive education we endured, it turns out that grandma was the one who least followed the good customs…how are we going to support the false morality and sexual repression that seem to be the pillars or our lives? What are we going to do with the contradictions? How are we going to confront the evidence that human beings are designed to have sexual attraction and the wild repression pitted against human nature will tend to search its natural course? The problem is that if we must review the authenticity of what grandma Matilde told us, what our own mother, a legion of devout aunts, and our own internalized repression we exert over our children, told us…then we will be forced to tear apart this set of ethics, we will find ourselves in such an uncomfortable place…that we will finally decide to stop questioning anything. We will accept that our mother was born after six months in the womb and that is that.

Often, during the process of the construction of the **human biography**, the individual may panic when we unfold the cards of a possible scenario and the HBr questions some "assumed" issues, deeply rooted in the official family discourse. It is not worth arguing. Just observe. Unfailingly, the reality will manifest itself.

However, it is not so bad that the individual defends his mother. It is understandable, he must be ready to "take apart" the fictitious construction that has provided **refuge**. It becomes complicated because we begin to realize that the family communication system has been altered. Lies have short legs, even when we live within deceived situations for many generations. It is not just grandma's pregnancy that was hidden, or grandpa's extramarital affairs or the suicide of a father of whom we have few memories, who passed into history as someone who died from heart disease (at the end we all die from the heart). The cover-ups will increase over time to support this system of misrepresentation of reality, so that those who command the family power can continue to act with some degree of freedom.

Every day we breath, live, and learn these "systems". If mom steals money from dad, because he is a drunkard and he squanders his salary gambling, and the children are witness, we will be given permission to lie, cheat and falsify. Our own mother has taught us to lie. Thus, we learn to live under these rules, which offer us some immediate benefits.

When reality has been permanently misrepresented and when we have clear memories of these facts and awareness that what happened does not coincide with what the adults named, we learn to fit reality to what is convenient to us. We will have to learn to lie, manipulate, deceive, seduce, delude…, so that we can adapt things in our favor. This occurrence is much more common than we imagine. During the process of the **human biographies**, the most arduous work is the "tearing apart" of the rooted beliefs and discourses we repeat "automatically".

Children are common victims of deceits, mostly because the adults believe that the children should not know what is happening. We should not be surprised at the level of disconnection and untruth we have learned to live with.

It is difficult to unravel the weave created by a system of lies and deceits, particularly when we observe it in a global manner. However, it is possible to perform this thoroughly within each individual's history: to compare the child's real and concrete experiences with the distorted discourses we have heard and accepted all our lives. This task cannot be postponed: it is the re-casting of the "puzzle" based on what truly happened, discarding what was told, which does not fit the scenario's logic.

To grow up and develop within a system of lies and secrets leaves us in absolute abandonment, because we do not have any trustworthy points of reference. Later, not only other people will not be trustworthy, but we do not consider ourselves to be trustworthy either. Including our perceptions and our emotions. When we become adults and are in the middle of a life crisis we attempt to peek into our own reality, we cannot find a sure signal. This is one of the reasons why we ask here and there for advice. Even worse, we believe what anyone tells us.

It is likely that we will live our lives with a high degree of confusion, without suspecting that this confusion present in every daily act has its origin in the lies that were established in our early childhood, and in some cases were upheld by several members of our family. Sometimes it happens in adoption cases, when the entire family has witnessed the adoption but systematically denies the child who is asking about his origins to have access to the truth. Paradoxically, the neighbors, the teachers, the school children know it...but not the adopted child, who is the only interested party. This modality of withholding access to the truth has been trivialized in our society, to the point where most of us come from family histories where lies and secrets were common currency, but we don't consciously register these facts. Neither we understand the extent of the emotional damage these fallacies and deceits have inflicted on our psychic development.

I am telling you one more time, the purpose for the construction of the **human biography** is, in principle, to reach out for the truth. The truth needs to coincide with the internal experience of the individual and the scenario in which he plays his relationships in life. We are not trying to divide between the good ones and the bad ones, or between innocents and sinners. No. We need to find the logic and we need to name with real words what happened and continues to happen. By observing a real scenario, the adult can make conscious decisions. This is all. It is a complex, stripped-down task, and loving as few.

The power of the maternal discourse

Where should we start? How can we detect the organization of this discourse both others' and our very own? Is it possible that our mother did not impose on us a discourse?

Where to start? From childhood

Usually, individuals come to a psychological consultation because we have some "urgent cannot-be-postponed" issues. For example, someone is concerned because if his fifteen-year-old child does not change behavior, he will be expelled from school. Or perhaps the individual's spouse was diagnosed with a breast tumor and wants to know how to accompany her. A couple comes to the consultation with great disagreement about absolutely everything and they want to come to a common decision about the children's education. Another one cannot understand why he is unfaithful to his spouse when he loves her. Here comes a woman without the desire to live. An older woman is worried about her depressed and idiotic daughter after years of ingesting antipsychotic medication. Another woman wants to wean her child. An older man wants to find purpose to his life, because he misplaced it. Well, we are all asking for help.

Most interestingly is that we expect to receive it in the form of a "solution" wrapped in pretty paper with a bow. We could offer that. We could tell the individual some nice, common-sense words. However, in our case we will always, always, always offer to navigate the experience of constructing his **human biography**. Why do we take on all this work? It is too much! The individual may say: "I have done therapy all my life". However, if he is not able to observe his own scenario from outside his miniscule point of view, we do not have another option. On the other hand, how could we help someone we don't know? At least we should introduce ourselves in this lifetime, let us observe together everything we can see and then we should observe some more, and in any event, after so much observing, the individual will be in a better position to make decisions, whichever they may be, to the benefit of his life and his environment.

Where should we start? At least, with the individual's **childhood**. If possible, including some information about the parents, grandparents or family of origin. It is not important if the mother is named Josefa or the father Manuel. What is important is to know what region of the world they come from, what socioeconomic environment, if they come from the country or the city, what religion or moral system they upheld. We need a panorama of broad strokes about the scenario where the plot will be developed.

Once we establish the context where our individual was born (as it is possible that five other siblings were born before him), we will search above anything else, throughout his childhood, the level of "mothering" he received. Why do we need this? Because his consciousness -and therefore his memories- will be organized based on the level of **emotional protection** or **emotional abandonment** he received. If he received enough protection -something difficult to find in our civilization- the memories will flow easily. Most likely this was not the reality of the individual's childhood. Therefore, the memories are tinged with that which was **named during childhood**. In nearly every case here will appear **the mother's discourse**.

Here we find the greatest difficulty. We are all accustomed to "talk" during therapy, to tell what happens to us. The "psy" professionals are accustomed to listen what the individual is telling. However, as detectives, we will have to "disjoint" the tales, because they are organized based on what mom said and repeated over the years. Then? What should we ask? How should we ask?

Contradictions within the official story

Let's start with childhood. The most frequent answer is: "Everything was normal". This information is of little value. To all of us, what we experienced during childhood is "normal", because our familial world was "the world we knew". Therefore, the HBrs will need to formulate more specific questions, related to the care we received: Who accompanied you to go to sleep? Who read you a story? Who prepared the food you liked best? Who knew what you were afraid of? Who would take you to school? Who helped you when you had a problem? Who spent time with you during your free time? Who offered you creative games? It is possible that there are no memories -which is a piece of data- or there are confused or contradictory images. If there are no memories, it is because no one close adult accompanied you nor offered empathy, understanding, affection or availability. If little children we do not receive help, support, love, closeness, caresses, understanding and a compassionate gaze, "this" we cannot obtain by ourselves. This is called **emotional abandonment** during childhood. Understand we are not talking about anything extreme. What happens is that nobody mentions the emotional abandonment. Because it is not named, it cannot be organized by our consciousness. That is, children do not have consciousness of our emotional abandonment, even if in our insides the fear and the loneliness pulse. This "never named" ends up in the "shadow". In the shadow, the emotional abandonment continues to exist.

Of course, this investigation is never lineal, but it is usually filled with contradictions. For example, the individual does not have any memories of anyone accompanying him to school, to the contrary, he remembers that he walked to school alone and returned from school alone. He also mentioned that: "mom stopped working when I was born to take care of me". Then we need to point out: "If you were a single child, and mom did not work, why did you walk to school alone at the age of six? Something does not fit. This is frequent because the child's emotional reality rarely matches what our mother told us.

We have a six-year-old child walking to school alone and a mother who stopped working to take care of him. We can then ask him about that period of his life: Did you like to go to school? Did you have friends? Do you remember any specific teacher? It is possible that the individual responds: "I was very timid, that is why I did not like to go to school. Sometimes I got hives and I was ashamed. There was a group of children that bullied me." The next question should be: "who was aware that there was a group of children that bullied you?". Here we have the first surprise. The individual realizes, now at forty-years old, that no one knew of his suffering. It is catastrophe at age six, to go to school with fear every day. This is called

emotional abandonment. This is called loneliness.

We begin by mentioning the distance separating the maternal discourse: "Mom stopped working to take care of me" and the reality that still pulses inside: "I was afraid". In this case, which is very common, it is obvious that the mother repeated: "I only took care of you", which from the mother's point of view must have been true. But from the child's point of view of his reality and his need for protection, no. Here we begin to perceive the two points of view (the mother's and the child's). While navigating the construction of the **human biography** we are interested in rescuing **the point of view of the child this individual has been**.

This was a child without siblings and lonely. We do not know what the mother did all day. Therefore, we should ask: "What did your mother do?" "Did she take care of the house?" "And your father?". "He was a merchant and worked a lot". "How was the relationship between them?". "Pretty bad, because my father was very violent". "Do you remember?". "No, but I know that he drank and then would hit my mother". "Do you remember any such event?". "Yes, I remember my mother always crying". "Do you remember your father being drunk?". "No, because my parents separated when I was three years old". "Ah! Three years old?".

The power of the maternal discourse

Here we find ourselves one more time, with the forcefulness of **the maternal discourse's power**. Whatsoever the mother mentioned becomes automatically the lens through which the child is in contact with reality. A distorted reality. This is a fundamental point. Let's observe that the adult organizes his childhood memories based on what his mother named and told her over many years, long after the father had already left the family. The context is heavily influenced by the mother's point of view. Regardless, we will attempt to build the scene in the most objectively possible manner.

Let's return to our protagonist, we will ask: "Are these your memories of your father beating your mother?". He will respond: "They are not my memories, but I believe my mother".

This is not about believing mom's word. It is about observing with utmost honesty the real scenario in which we grew up. For now, the memories are influenced by what mom has named throughout our childhood. If dad separated from mom when the individual was three years old, it is unlikely that the father's point of view has any place in this scenario. What is clear is that mom cried and named her own hurt. We also know that our individual was **alone**. We will have to continue asking questions, taking in consideration the chronology of the events.

Why is it important to follow the chronology? Because our consciousness will "skip over" the memories it cannot process. Interestingly, what the individual does not remember is exactly what is of most interest to us. We take a disciplined approach during the investigation -taking into account the chronology of facts (events, ages, specific circumstances) to help us not to miss some important clues and find out what he does not remember,

Let's continue with our example. We would pose more punctual questions: "If your parents separated when you were three years old, and your mother did not work, who supported the household?". "I think it was my father". "Did your mother remarry?". "No, she was not able to trust anyone again".

Who spokes those phrases? Mom, of course. In the mind of this child, dad is bad, unforgivable, on the other hand, mom is good and suffers. However, nobody mentions what is happening to the child, even as the child knows everything that happens to mom. This is important because the mother did not name the child's loneliness, or his infantile difficulties, repressed desires, nor his fears or whatever this child experienced. Instead, she named in detail her own emotional states. This provides a panorama; we could draw a picture of this childhood showing this **child looking at his mother** and knowing everything about her suffering. We will share this with the individual.

We will work with the image (even if this is a bit shocking) of a child being devoured by a crocodile.

The client is moved and says: "This is correct. I have never thought about it like this". We have now confirmed -because the individual agreed- that we have a child being swallowed by his mother, a child who obviously looks at his mom, but who inversely is not sufficiently seen by her. At this point, like the detectives we are, we shall think about how the story can continue. With a little bit of training, it is not too difficult. What can happen to a child who is not seen and who satisfies every maternal need? First, he can be in harm's way because there is nobody near him with sufficient emotional availability to care for him. What can happen to a child in danger? Everything. From small obstacles to great abuses. Since we are imagining and making up this case, I will not make it too dire, but common. We will have to ask him what happened when he was a child, approaching with earnestness, the small and large sufferings his mother never saw.

Devoured by mom

What should we ask? For example, how was he able to resolve the relationships with the children in school, with his teachers, with the studies, with any activities in which he would have wanted to participate. Asking with patience, he will remember a gang of older children who would steal his lunch and would take away his school supplies. We ask him if his mother knew about this. "No, it never occurred to me to tell her about this". We continue to confirm, it is terrible for a young child to be the subject of the mistreatment from older children, but **it is much worse that mom does not know** and that he felt he did not have the right to bother her with his unimportant things.

Words that fit

We will talk about all of this with the client. Little by little the memories will appear in gushes, since we have named the **loneliness** and the gaze we scarcely received. The scenes we experienced fit with the word "loneliness" and the word "fear"; since they fit, our consciousness can "bring them back" because there is a place where we can organize them. Since they have not been named before, our consciousness could not "remember".

Our childhood memories are like a room covered in an impenetrable mountain of disorderly clothes. It is impossible to find anything in this chaos. But if we decide to place a shelf labeled "pants", we will possibly look for pants in the middle of this mountain of clothes. First, we can only find two or three. We fold them tidily; we place them on the shelf, and we look for them again. Soon we will be better trained to continue finding more pants peeking in between the colorful fabrics. We will organize them. Days later, we will place a second shelf labeled "long

117

sleeve shirts"; surprisingly, we will recognize them amid this chaos. We will select them one by one; we will fold them and place them on their shelf. We will do the same with the socks, the ties and the hats. As soon as there is a shelf with the corresponding label, it will be easier to detect the pieces of clothing that need to find their place.

Our consciousness works similarly; when the HBr offers a shelf and a label, for example: "Fear of the dark"; at the beginning we do not find any fear, but once we detect one, there is an organized place (a shelf) that helps us discover the other ones. This process helps the individual "get in touch" with experiences which, since they had not been named until now, did not have "any shelf" where to come to light. When we begin to name certain internal realities, for example, the distance we felt as children from the world of adults, the "memories" come pouring out. We remember more and more instances of our loneliness, isolation or sadness. Because we can organize them in their respective "shelves".

Coming back to our case and not to bore you too much, we will traverse different experiences occurred during his childhood: related to school, his loneliness, mom, mom's words, his environment..., and find what other pieces fit in this puzzle of childhood experiences, from the place of the emotional abandonment he lived.

There is a fundamental question to be asked at this juncture: "What did mom say about you?". "That I was a good boy, very intelligent and that I was going to be a doctor". In this instant, mom dressed him up in his suit. In order to respond to mom's desire, he was going to have to be a good boy, intelligent, or at least studious. We can draw our hypothesis of good and studious child, but we will ask to confirm: "Did you do well in school?". "Yes, I never created any problems, my mom never had to help me with homework". Mom must have been happy with such a good child who did not create any problems and allowed her to "show" him off with pride. Of course, even if it is difficult to realize it now, mom was only worried about herself, not about her real child. We were saying that mom was happy with this child. Not that this child was happy with his life.

Fitting within our character

Continuing with the timeline, the time arrives to talk about adolescence. During adolescence, we complete the design of the character. The individuals "steps out into the world" as it were, dressed in our costume to fulfill our role as best we can. The questions we will pose will be related to the maternal discourse, that is the costume in which the mother dressed up the child.

As I explained earlier, I understand adolescence as a second birth. This is the second time during our life when there is an **explosion of vitality** that brings the youngster in front of his own strength. Adolescence is the time when we can manifest our essential being, if the mother has not squeezed out of this child his being's most precious essence. The youngster's vital pulse will be manifested in two realms: sexual desire and vocation. Along the construction of the **human biography**, it is important to approach both subjects, always following the same hypothesis. Let's be good detectives and think clearly before asking any questions to the individual.

Let's play a game. What do you think will happen with his vocation? Possibly he has already resolved the issue, since mom said he was intelligent and that he would make an excellent physician. "Having it resolved" in this

119

case seems like a joke. This is no true vocation. This is **submissiveness to the maternal desire**. Let's remember that mom wanted her child to become a doctor; it is possible that he will "choose" the medical profession. We understand that in this **human biography**, there is no "election". The only one who chooses is mom, the only one deserving of such privilege. It is possible that our individual will assure us that he always liked medicine. We will not contradict him, because effectively, he feels that it was his own election.

Let's assume that he goes through his career without much trouble, fulfilling mom's desires to the end. In this case -if he is so libidinally aware of mom- the affectionate relationships with women will be complicated, because here he would be in clear competition with mom. In any case, to cover the scenes most completely, we always need to confirm our hypothesis. Until now, we know that mom gazes at herself, that our individual was a solitary child, there were no siblings or father present, he liked to read... and little else. We discuss his vocation and there are no cracks. Later we discuss friendship or love relationships, knowing that he arrives at this place with little training, and in addition, he worries about mom.

If, when we ask for information about relationships with women, the answers are vague, it is worthwhile asking about what worried him most about his mother during his college years. Perhaps he will tell us that "during that period" his mother was ill. We need to find more details. Perhaps he will explain: "Mi mother started with panic attacks, she had to take medication, it was complicated, because they had to change medication several times, it was several years until she was diagnosed with bipolar disease". Etc. This confirms our hypothesis. Mom -now with an adult son-continues to devour him. The young man remains emotionally abused by his mother and has just enough libido left for his studies and then for his work. Now we look again at the picture of the gigantic crocodile jaw eating this tender child.

This is a run of the mill story. A young man with good intentions, intelligent, a gentleman and alone. We will share this panorama with the client. There is nothing new for him, but perhaps the novelty is in the perspective of observing his own scenario. The image fits.

The detective's hypotheses

At some point, even if late, he will begin to have experiences with women. We will attempt to approach each of those experiences and fit them within the general plot. If we were to pose a hypothesis, what type of women will feel attractive to him? Perhaps demanding women, needy, with great personal conflicts, who are fascinated by his patience and ability to listen, of this affectionate, gentle and docile man. What woman would not fall in love with a man who can listen? Here we have our hero, he is beginning to experience love relationships with women, accumulating experiences and discovering love's delights.

At this point we need to show him something important: he is loved to the extent that he listens and **is at the service** of the difficulties of the woman of the day. Who does she remind us of? His mom, of course, who also loves him, but holds him submissive to her desires.

Let's assume that our client gets married to a woman, a colleague at the hospital. After exhausting stories of women who demanded much, he found exactly what he was searching in his current partner: someone relatively self-sufficient who does not need others' energy to live in harmony. They have a good relationship, they have common interests, and they live a quiet life. Both love to work, research and sports. They have a simple and peaceful routine. We arrive at the current time. Why is he requesting a consultation? Because three years ago they decided to have children and his wife is not getting pregnant. They have done all the tests and the only result is a slow mobility in his sperm, but nothing too alarming. There are no physiological reasons or any pathology. His wife insists in starting IVF treatment, he is resisting the idea because of the cost. They do not have the money.

What should we do? We will look at the entire scenario (remember we are working with the **image of a child being eaten by his mother**). We will ask how is the mother doing right now? He will tell us that she is worse than ever, she is pressuring him to live with them and the only disagreements he has with his wife are about this subject. We talk about his daily routine, and we find out that the individual visits his mother every day, before returning home from work. He also tells us that he pays for a daytime caregiver and a nighttime and weekend caregiver.

Is it wrong for a single child to care for his ailing mother? Should he abandon her? No. It is not our place to judge what the individual decides. Each one decides what to do with his life as best he can. Beyond any moral conundrum, we understand that the mother -depressed since ancient times- abusive and "thief" of her son's vital energy (her only child, because she does not take the energy shared among several), has left him devoid of libido to be able to produce a child of his own.

Are we certain? No, this is only an idea. We have a forty-year-old man, who has done everything right: he is a hard worker, honest, and intelligent. Today he wishes to have a child with his wife and cannot get her pregnant. All his vital energy -blind and unconsciously- will be swallowed by his mother who will continue to take and hoard his economic, affective and emotional resources... until he is empty and exhausted.

The individual asks, what should he do? We do not know. At least we have placed all the cards on the table. He looks at them, holds his head between his hands while repeating: "This is it; this is it; this is it".

Perhaps our work is finished, perhaps we ask him if he wishes we continue accompanying him. What we have accomplished is to compare the **maternal discourse** which held him completely enclosed within his mother's wishes against the **lived experience of his essential being**, of his internal being or whatever you want to call it. Once this has been spoken, he will be in a better position to make personal decisions. By looking at the entire picture. Perhaps starting IVF treatments to become pregnant may not be the first option to be considered. Perhaps this may be the right moment to have an honest conversation with his spouse about these complex realities that affect her as well, more than he would have imagined. He may be able to look at himself and recognize the loss of energy that slips away since ancient times, to satisfy his mother. Whatever he is going to do, if he can find resolution by observing the complete scenario, he is likely to have more opportunities to change the rules of the game in everyone's favor, even his mother.

This is a made-up example -which I have used to explain how to detect the maternal discourse and how to compare it with the internal reality- is one among thousands. Everyone brings a specific universe of relationships. The art lies in being able to discover the "internal plot" instead of being fascinated by and developing interpretations within the repeated stories that each individual carries in his backpack of the "official story".

How to detect the deceived discourse?

We all observe reality through a subjective and partial crystal. In fact, there are no "objective views". However, it is important to understand through which lens are we looking; this will determine "what we see". In all cases, this lens has been "installed" during childhood. Therefore, it is important to observe the events without losing sight of the lens color through which the client remembers, feels, or connects with reality.

Thus, before trying to solve any specific problem, it is important to look at our lens. Our mind was organized by the words emoted by someone when we were children. Or, our mind was crazed, if "that" which was named was too far removed from our tangible experiences. Even in those cases, it will be a relief to name with new words the events of the past, because we will be finally able to understand the causes of our historical unease, our "feeling off" or our permanent confusion.

Do all individuals carry inside a history disconnected between what was told and what was experienced? Unfortunately, it is rare to find a case when it does not happen. It is not worth tackling other issues before clearly understanding what lens the individual is using to see himself and others.

All our beliefs, thoughts, judgements, preferences and lifestyles are organized based on a collection of sayings proffered by someone during our early childhood. Even if we feel to have been historically standing on the opposite side of the street from our parents, to have never agreed with their point of view or their backwards lifestyle. If this were the case, then our parents have, in some way, named our opposition, our rebellion or our expulsion. Therefore, we will also have a name. Often our parents bestow upon us the title of rebel without a cause and then we believe throughout our adult lives that we devote our lives fighting for noble causes. Thus, we present ourselves to society: as revolutionaries, showing off the pride of our valor and spunk. But it could happen…that searching thoroughly within our true lives, we may not find a thread of courage or heroism; we are simply repeating our mother's or our father 's deceived discourse, believing we are "that" which they have named.

In any case, it is necessary to discover if what we have named today about ourselves fits with reality or if we continue to repeat what we have heard infinite times during our childhood. In these cases, let's build the puzzle of our lives based on a genuine, honest and personal path.

Does the deceived discourse always belong to the mother? In most cases, yes. But in some cases, the father's discourse takes precedence. Or the grandmother's discourse, if she has been an important figure and she has directed the comings and goings of the family. It is also possible in some families that the siblings are divided, some are aligned with our mother's discourse, and some are aligned with our father's discourse. In these cases, most likely there have been emotional battles lasting many years and each parent took some of the children as hostages for their own benefit. It is understandable that some of us ended up in one trench and others on the opposite side, with the ensuing hate and rancor among the siblings. Later we will look at some examples for better understanding.

It is important to understand in who's voice we are speaking, through which lens we are looking, and what discourse we have unknowingly adopted, to draw the complete scenario and discover where the threads of the most important family subjects are. In any war, obvious or hidden, we need to know which side each character is aligned with. This is fundamental to understanding why he thinks as he does about the grandmother, the brother, the mother, the teacher, and his political, economic, and philosophical opinions.

Soon we will understand that our "personal opinions" are not so personal. Most of the time, they fit the discourse of our "deceived ego", even if we believe we have conceived them in freedom. Each character has a role to fulfill; this role fits within a specific location within the scenario and has a script to recite.

Is it possible that our mother has not imposed on us any discourse at all?

We all love our mothers. Our mother is an exception to the rule, and we assume that she -who has been so good- has not imposed on us any discourse at all. It is difficult to recognize what character we have adopted; it is even more complex to recognize the engine that powers our actions and to understand what role we have taken within our environment. Could it be that we are not trapped? Are we all subject to the maternal discourse? Are there exceptions?

In order not to be held in the places selected by the maternal discourse, we would have to be raised with freedom and beyond the projections of our parents. For this to happen, we need to have had parents willing to observe themselves, to observe their own shadow and to take responsibility for the less brilliant and less valued aspects of themselves.

The exercise of daily self-inquiry

In an ideal world, our parents would have understood that if they truly want to convey to us a less conditioned life, they need to inquire their own emotional history, questioning without fear its emotional origins. What does it mean to inquire about our own personal history? To recognize our shadow, with help. To be willing to enter the painful fields that have been forgotten by our consciousness. Knowing that as adults, we will find sufficient resources to confront the events happened during our childhoods, to live searching for the profound sense of our existence.

If our mother could have reviewed her history and recognized that she was raised by an infantile, egocentric mother, little able to offer her a loving place in her life, perhaps our mother may not have been able to avoid the pain, however she could have understood her own mother, and by understanding herself, she could decide to mature to be able to raise us, our siblings and us, instead of pretending to continue to be nourished by us as an adult.

If our mother, at any time in her life, decided to look at her own reality just as it is, it means that she entered adulthood. Later, perhaps, she could take on an attitude of opening and introspection, perhaps searching for a teacher or a guide to shed light, paying attention to what her friends, colleagues and family members point at, especially when it is less than beautiful. She will also pay attention to us, her children, relentless plaintiffs of the soul's darkness.

If this had been our mother's ongoing intention, perhaps she could live on the razor's edge of her conscious capability to raise her own children. What children need most, is parents who can question themselves in the most honest manner. When the adults can observe our entire maps and our own automated responses organized within the lack of love, we will be able to look at ourselves with a more open mind and fewer prejudices. Instead of interpreting everything the child is doing, instead of closing ourselves in characters that calm them, we could carefully name what is truly happening, with simple, clear words. The adults could also share with us what happens to them, because we are all part of one complex emotional universe.

Thus, the heart of adults and children alike, the internal experiences, the sensations, and the perceptions will have a real "place" where to manifest…instead of having to fit them within a preconceived scenario. If this would have happened, if when we were children instead of hearing: "How lazy you are, just like your father", they would have asked us "Do you not want to go to school? Is it because other children bother you?", then it would have been very different. In this case we would not have dressed in the costume of the "lazy one who does not mind his parents", nor any other costume. Perhaps we had a problem we did not know how to resolve or express. But if we were lucky to have an adult who could name what was happening to us and could help us tackle a problem too complex for us…we would not have needed to wear any costume: not the lazy one, nor the brave or the decisive one.

Of course, to inquire within requires daily training and permanent personal questioning. It is effortful and engaging; it may take us years to implement so that it can become automatic. Perhaps the reader believes it is exaggerated to pretend something like this from our mother, poor mother, she came from the post-war era and led a sacrificed life. We should unequivocally recognize that, without the availability of self- inquiry, she was forced to display on us the entire gamut of deceived discourses that had helped her survive.

I want to emphasize that it does not matter that our mother "did everything correctly". It does not matter if she was a fantastic mother, warm, patient, sacrificed or vigilant. Our need was to be raised on the axis of our essential being and in profound connection with our own selves, meaning **that our mother would have needed to understand herself.** If we did not have an adult and mature mother, who understands her own emotional states and her own emotional thread, she could not pour her wisdom over us. Therefore, it is unlikely that we were able to confront life in a state of total consciousness.

To become adults is to hold the reins of our lives, to traverse the woods to confront our internal demons, to look at them in the eye and to decide at the end of this perilous path, which is our own path. From this point on, we will be totally responsible for the decisions we make in all areas of our lives, including the ability not to imprison our children-if we have them- in the characters that are functional to us. It is possible to look at our children, to look at our partners, to look at our siblings, to look at our neighbors, if we have previously been able to look at our own entire scenarios, if we have had the courage to doubt the official discourse and if we can decide to exit from our prison naked, and to tear away the infantile structure. Perhaps then, we can ask the children what they need from us, instead of imposing with authority that they adapt to our needs and force them to carry indefinitely the heavy backpack of someone else's desires.

I am sorry if someone is disappointed. Until now, I have not found a single individual who does not carry the maternal incapacity to take care of her own abandonment shifting it onto us when we were children. Thus – and exactly because of this- those of us who are adults today, we have a new opportunity, the opportunity to inquire within ourselves and to access that which we still do not know about ourselves.

The "deceived self"

Inquiring into our own deceived story

It does not matter what is the apparent reason for the initial consultation, it does not matter whether it is urgent, whether it is a man or a woman, it does not matter if the client thinks that we have all the solutions and only we are able to understand. We can help the individual if we walk together and honestly along his life story -and if possible- the lives of his forefathers and relatives – to integrate his shadow. This is what the "organization of the **human biography**" is all about. As I have said earlier, among the HBrs that practice in my team, we lovingly call the **human biography "**HB" (aitch bee). We come back to the HBs once and again, each time we get lost in tales and complains the individual believes are necessary to understand his problem.

The urgency to resolve what preoccupies us leaves us anxious and neglectful to remember all those events that happened long ago. In Argentina, where most people have already had some "psy" experience, we are even less inclined. In those cases, we ask the client to define in a few phrases the salient points of his past therapeutic work, to take advantage of it and deepen it a bit more. Seldom the individuals have a clear understanding about the work they have done. Most often we say: "The therapist accompanied me during the grieving of my father's death" or "few people know me as well as he does". Very well, this is not very helpful. We are forced to start from the beginning: the childhood experiences. Which experiences? The ones the individual remembers? No. Because the memories are tinged with what mom has said. However, we will have to find, as detectives, the level of "mothering" he received. The real one, not the one he was told. This joint search requires more art than intelligence. More training than preconceived ideas.

Let's suppose that we decide to construct our **human biography**; first appears a common challenge, we will respond from the point of view of the established character. He had his deceived discourse already prepared. The primary obstacle when attempting to organize a **human biography** is the identity, the role in which we "recognize ourselves", which is led by our "conscious self", our character. We present ourselves to the world in a certain manner, believing "this is who we are".

An efficient woman

For example: I am an executive assistant: efficient, punctual, intelligent, decisive, impatient, demanding and responsible. It is possible that all these qualities are true. But this is not what is of interest to us, but what happens when I place in motion my demanding and efficient side. We will search for the suffering of those around us. For example, if I am proud of my great professional results, I will have a hard time tolerating the ineptitude, carelessness or distractions of others. It is likely that to "feed" my character I will unconsciously surround myself with particularly forgetful or inattentive people. Thus, I am certain of holding the power in the realm of efficiency. If this is my character, it is possible that the affective universe may feel boring, and the autonomy with which I handle the more concrete aspects of my life may be more exciting.

Why would she come to the consultation? Perhaps because the children misbehave in school, even if they are treated by psychologists. Being decisive, I want an immediate solution.

I am sorry to insist on the same concept, but we explain to our energetic and competent individual that we will start by asking about her birth and earliest memories of childhood. If we are the individual, we will say: "I was born awake". "Who said that?". "What do you mean by who said that? All my family said that!" "Someone said it first, probably your mother". "Yes, of course, all my life my mother said that I was born awake and that I paid attention to everything, I did not miss anything, I was a firecracker".

After we have listened to thousands of stories, it may seem funny, but the individuals name with candor, the character they have inhabited. Even if certain characters can have a positive or glamorous side, we will agree that it is a heavy burden for a little girl to sustain "to be always awake". No child is ever "born awake". What I mean is that it is not the role of a child to be permanently alert. He does it because he does not have a choice.

The maternal discourse says: "How wonderful, she was attentive and perceptive", but we add: "There was also a good amount of neglect and emotional abandonment, and the incapacity of your mother to care for you when you were a baby". How do we know? If we are good detectives, we will know from what the mother has said. However, our individual adopts and defends the maternal discourse. From that moment on, it stops being the maternal discourse and becomes the discourse of the "deceived I". She will say: "I perfectly remember how much attention I paid to everything" There is no doubt. Mom put the costume on her, dictated the script and the girl made it her own.

As we continue our inquiry, we will ask to confirm the mother's need to have her little child assume responsibilities, since "she was born awake", that is, mature. Effectively, memories will appear where she is taking care of her brothers at a very tender age, fighting for just causes in school, hoisting a flag or defending her convictions to the end. Obviously, she will have followers and detractors as well. This is the law of a complete scenario. In this vein, we will be most interested in the detractors, which initially our individual will despise. "What does it matter what those idiots thought?" says the leader character. It is of interest to us, because it is likely that what happened to those "idiots" was the same that happened to the siblings who were on the opposite trench of the family battles during childhood. Let's imagine that the mother was also an energetic, strong and decisive woman.

These are additional reasons for our heroine to identify with her mother and settle in the intelligent character her mother gifted her when she was born. We can try something: let's ask her something about the mother. Her eyes will shine telling us some story about this exceptional mother (perhaps she was). What we are looking for is confirmation that the mother and the daughter were on the same team, in the entrepreneurs' team. Perhaps mom did not work, even if she despised the father, who financially supported the family for over fifty years. We should know that the owner of the official discourse has the power of the "truth" (which may not be so, but we will reveal this later). We are talking about the power of the discourse, in this case the maternal discourse.

Let us inquire about the emotional reality of the characters that remained on the other trench, the trench of the "ineffective": the father and the siblings. Our individual has much to say about them: my youngest brother was a "disaster", my parents did not know where else to send him to school. The one in the middle did not talk, we used to say that the mice stole his tongue. He did not have any friends. Today, he has not changed, he lives alone with two cats. My two brothers are "unpresentable". Is this true? Depends on who's point of view we use. Obviously, this is the point of view of our audacious and arrogant character.

In every HB we travel through the scenes without abandoning the chronology. We arrive at her adolescence. If we play "futurology", it is easy to imagine that she destroyed everyone's desire. Remember that we are detectives. We draw certain hypothesis for our investigation; however, it is necessary to confirm now and again. Effectively she had a period of *femme fatale,* sure of herself, entrepreneurial, ready to step on anyone to reach her goals. With this type of character, it is possible to climb the corporate ladder, but we remain very lonely in the emotional realm. The questions that will direct our individual to connect with this "other side" is related to the intimate emotional relationships. There will be weak men, drug users that needed saving or males seduced by her expression, later becoming jealous or competitive. How did her relationships begin? With men fascinated by our heroine. How did the relationships end? Unfailingly with significant violence. Our protagonist resembles the Red Queen in the movie *Alice in Wonderland* with Tim Burton: each time she did not like something, she would order: "Off with his head!". We could show her an image (see in the following chapters about the importance of images in the construction of the **human biographies**).

Each character's point of view

The largest obstacle we encounter when we enter the life histories, is that the "character" thinks he is right. The "conscious I" does not take into consideration other points of view. Thus, we name it the "deceived I", because of all the "I's" is the one who least understands objectively. It is the part of ourselves that believes itself to be most sharp - like the king's favorite son in any fairytale- however, he knows nothing about life. Thus, he fails over and over again. This "deceived I", defends his own point of view, considering it the only and the best.

I insist, when we are constructing a **human biography**, what the individual is telling us, that is what the "deceived I" is proclaiming, is of no interest to us. Whatever the individual tells spontaneously during a therapeutic consultation, he tells it from the place of the "deceived I", and as such it cannot provide any valuable information. Therefore, we need to discard this information, even if it has impacted us or provided thorny or juicy descriptions that delight our senses. To use the imaginary example, it does not matter the details related to the regrettable episodes unfolded by ex-partners, brothers, employees or acquaintances of our individual, if they are interpreted by the "deceived I" of someone who believes she is infallible. We already know that from the point of view of the "deceived I", she will consider "stupid" anything that is not fast and efficient.

Chronologically, we are in front of a young woman, entrepreneurial, executive, and successful at work. In her relationships with men, she wields the power. Today, she is 45 years old, she is married, has two school-age sons and is coming to the consultation preoccupied about them. We will try to organize the information we have and investigate the sequence of events based on logic. Finally, we will arrive at her current concern.

Genius vs imbeciles

Finally, who is she going to have as a life partner? With a weak man like many she dated, which she either had to save or despise? It is also possible that she enters a relationship with a strong man, with whom she can ally against the rest of the world. If there are many enemies outside, stupid, inept, unproductive, it will be easy to establish an ironlike alliance. Obviously, these movements are unconscious, but they work. To find out which was her choice, we will have to ask her, first searching for the "type" of couple. There are no half measures with our heroine, she will be able to respond immediately if her husband is a "genius" or an "imbecile". Let's assume she selected a strong and decisive man like herself. Let us also assume that this man is a high-level executive and they met in the business world.

Along the meetings for the construction of the HB we will name the emotional abandonment she experienced during her entire childhood, the need to mature at age six or seven years, the responsibility to make decisions at a very tender age and above all the belief that when she was a girl, she was the only one who could properly fulfill her mother's needs. If we can "touch" this needy child outside of the "deceived I's" discourse, we could enter a very interesting journey. If we are not able, we won't.

Our purpose is to show the benefits and the disadvantages or the price each character must pay, because the cost is something the individual feels, but often cannot see.

We all pay our price, feeling unease and never understanding what we could do to feel better. We suffer inside the burden of supporting our character because we cannot detect it with clarity. In this case, the price to pay could have been an enormous loneliness, great distrust, and the belief that the world is made up of useless people who will never be able to help us. It is very difficult to live believing that the world turns only because we move it... From this perspective, we will never trust another person, or delegate in another...All this belongs to the individual's "shadow". We spend our lives despising others, but we are unable to speak of the anguish we experience by having to dig a daily trench between us and the rest of the world. Of course, we blame others for being unable to reach our homeland.

Let's assume that our individual is beginning to see this situation. When we name the distance that lays between her and nearly everyone else, she accepts, stammering: "I have never seen it in this light", or "It could be, I think so". Then we could draw a simple image, in which she and her husband are sitting at the top of a mountain, allies, holding hands, looking with disdain at the rest of humanity. It is a place that conveys power. It is also a solitary place. No one would dream that these gods would need anything from anyone. In this picture, the rest of us, we become incapable little subjects who have nothing to offer to the king and queen of this kingdom. There is distance. Godlikeness. Envy. Incomprehension. Rancor. Ignorance. Let's imagine a tall mountain, two individuals on their thrones up high and the rest of the world down below. It would be a good exercise to think about what is felt "up high" and what is felt "down below", because both

The reign

feelings are valid, relative to where we are standing on the "map".

Personally, when we get to this point, I would work on the "genius versus idiots" theme. Because the "deceived I" of this woman is clearly proud of her own "genius" and complains about having to deal daily with all the other secondary characters in this play, who assume the roles of stupid, clumsy or slow. Until such time as we can observe together how she has cast the each one of the characters' roles, she will be unable to understand what she is unconsciously generating in each one and will be unable to move the board-game tokens she helped design.

When this panorama becomes clear, we will be able to inquire about the birth of her children, the rearing, her bond with them, the changes in her emotional relationship with her husband, and the daily difficulties. In this case, we are dealing with a woman who works and has organized her identity around her professional success and emotional distance. We can assume that when she became a mother, many previously unimaginable difficulties appeared.

Futurology, an obvious subject

If we played "futurology" we would know that little children will become "a headache", since she is much more comfortable moving within the professional work environment than the subtle and emotional realms. The birth and coexistence with young children is difficult for everybody, but it will be particularly difficult for our individual. We all know that child-rearing and living with children is not resolved with efficacy, with concrete solutions and much less with speed. If we consider her character, we can assume that she felt trapped in an endless labyrinth.

Based on this understanding, we may need to stop and ask very specific questions about her children's early years. Why? Because they must have been very uncomfortable to her character; it is likely she will want to skip over saying "this happened a long time ago". Or perhaps she may have forgotten almost all the details of her babies' first years.

Therefore, our work must place special emphasis on this section of the story, that has become shadow. How do we ask the questions? With many details. Birth. First days. Puerperium. Breastfeeding.

Our heroine will respond automatically: "Everything was perfect, Johnny was an angel, he ate and slept". It is very unlikely. From the place of the "deceived I" this character arrived at the childbirth thinking she had everything under control. If there is a place where the control falls apart…that is the scene of childbirth. Let us assume she had a C-section. She will defend the modern theories of elective C-section, the umbilical cord wrapped or the perfect excuse not to connect with what happened to her. The more out-of-control experiences she tucked away in the shadow, the more we will need to search there. Let us think that the character will attempt, in the middle of the chaos, to return to the field she dominates, her professional work. Interestingly, if we ask her about her work during this period -for example, to whom she delegated her most pressing tasks, what she organized, etc.- she will tell us that during her first pregnancy she left her old job with a national firm to take a position entailing more responsibility in a multinational company with the possibility of advancement she had hoped for some time. The move to the new offices was taking place when her labor started. We can glimpse how she needed to divert her libido to new work projects and the possible lack of connection to the approaching labor and her baby's presence, she could hardly imagine until now.

This is the perfect moment to stop, rewind the stories, picking up from the marvelous and happy childbirth she said to have lived. In the middle of moving offices, with work projects at the peak of splendor, with promises to her employer of efficacy and pretending to give birth to a child with the same energy as she approaches work. Something does not fit. We could say that we imagine a chaotic scene. Silence. A few seconds later, for the first time, our individual begins to cry. She tries that we do not notice. We approach her physically without touching her yet. She looks uncomfortable. We ask some soft questions. Then she starts to wail, to cough, to blow her nose, while we attempt to hug her, we perceive that her entire body is trembling. She cries proffering incomprehensible words, that she is tired, that it is difficult, that her back hurts, that she needs a vacation, that the children do not recognize her efforts, that life is easier for men, and it is not fair. Very well, we have touched some of the shadowy material. We will stay here for a while.

The plain truth

We will search and name the events outside of the "deceived I's" discourse, that had formally organized everything. We return to the labor. The lack of any communication with the physician who was going to attend to her. The lack of personal research to find out something about medical attention during childbirth, assuming this belonged to a flimsy feminine universe she was not interested in. We see the disdain for anything that is soft, even in reference to women in labor. She has become one of those but prefers to sustain her usual character: efficient and powerful. She undergoes a C-section, but her character, strong and ambitious, with a frozen heart and a blank mind asks to walk herself to the operating room. Admirable. Brave.

Once the baby is born, they show the baby to her, they take it away, perform mechanically all the hospital routines, but she remains stoic, protected by her costume. Then she continues with the tale of the "deceived I" and says: "I did not have any milk, so I did not waste any time, the baby started taking formula right away, and it was fantastic". From now on, all the "fantastics" that we will hear from our individual will be taken with "a pinch of salt". This is the time to name with different words what had happened. We will say: "It was probably a shock to have a C-section, and to have your baby in your arms for the first time, perhaps you felt like he was a stranger, you may have asked yourself if you were a normal mother and whether you had any vestige of the famous maternal instinct, since you had ambivalent feelings about this baby. Perhaps a lot of people came in and out of your room with a lot of indications". Then, amazed at her own weakness, she will say crying: "Yes, yes, just like that, they would show me how to lift him, how to calm him. On top of everything, the scar was very painful; my husband was celebrating with champagne with his friends, and I wanted to kill him; the baby did not like it when I would put him at my breast, it was torture, and then I did not even want to hold him because as soon as I touched him, he would start crying, but with the nurses he would be calm".

We are now getting away from the "fantastic" from

a few minutes ago and we will continue to name the possible realities outside of her character's construction: It is possible that you did not imagine the time and silence you and your baby required, nor the calm and quiet needed to get to know each other. It may have been very difficult to enter a "time without time" when you had just begun a new job in a new company. Your external reality was very far from the connection and the baby's needs".

Most likely our individual will remember -after a few interventions-discussions with her husband, friends that were offering worthless advice, desire to run away from there, the oppression on her chest we can now name..., taking her to a chaos of sensations that she had until now disdained: worthless, lost, dripping, in pain, dislocated, disoriented. Disgusting.

We can look again at the image of the mountain, her queen's crown, we add a baby in arms. Rather than a baby...it will be an alien.

She will attend the following meeting a little bit more relaxed, dressed more informally, the hair down. This is a good sign. She relaxed. She remembered. For a short while she took off her mask that was hurting her; for a little while she trusteed us. We will be able to continue our investigation and the eagerness to bring to light those events she rejected and relegated to the shadow. We won't be surprised to know that five days after giving birth she was back at the office. Of course, she ran away in despair to her identity place. We are not going to judge whether she was or not a good mother, it does not concern us. The only thing that matters, from the point of view of her character, she did the only thing she knew how.

Introducing the child's point of view

Here our role changes: we need to **add the child's point of view**. We are required to introduce his voice, telling with simple words everything this five-day old, month old, two months old, four months old, six months old baby was living. His mother was disconnected from his basic needs, leaving him in the hands of surrogates, fed, cleaned, attended to, but **alone**. It is not worth talking about physical contact, nor emotional fusion, presence, emotional availability, emotional openness or silence. These concepts are unknown -not to say discredited- by our character. In the meantime, there is a baby who is going to ask for "mothering" in any way he can. It is possible that he gets sick. We will ask about illnesses. Our individual will automatically respond that he was "very healthy"; if we insist with more details, she will remember the bronchitis, bronchiolitis, the admissions to the hospital because of convulsions with high fevers, ear infections, never-ending colds, nights without sleep with nebulizers and other delights of nightlife with children at home. Of course, she had to work, therefore it is possible she does not have clear memories because by then she had hired a nurse to take care of the child at night.

We continue to name the experiences from the baby's point of view, and the enormous distance that was widening between the child's soul and the mom's soul. With patience, we will guide the memory of little anecdotes, offering its due attention to each one, not because they are important in themselves, but to allow her to emotionally register them, which is a new experience for her. This new awareness hurts. Since she is a very intelligent woman, she will joke about what she is discovering about herself,

145

laughing at herself and saying she never paid so much money to suffer. She knows that this new closeness to "the other side of herself" is painful, but extremely necessary.

Then we will approach the baby's first year, then the second. The second pregnancy and childbirth, probably like the first. The birth of her second son. She did not breastfeed either. More nannies. Less attention, since they were all trained on what to do with snot and fevers, the ear infections and the antibiotics. That is, we will look at the daily family life, with an entrepreneurial mother who works a lot, a father who also works a lot, two young children, who are alone, they get sick a lot and survive as best they can.

And the father?

I know that many readers will say at this point: and the father? Ah! Why the father is not providing care, he is not even present in the picture? Well…there could be a father that provides care, but in this scenario, the marital agreement was based on work, success, resolutions and activity. And to have enough money available. I am very sorry, but it is the role of the woman who became mother to play her other side. These babies brought something so emotionally intense -and so unknown to the character she embodies- that at this moment the woman was unable to understand it. Her interpretations were from the point of view of the successful character. With some luck, the children's father accompanied this point of view, since his character is like his wife's. He did not suffer because he did not give birth, did not have milk, did not have to unfold any sort of mothering. Therefore, he did not even crack. He accompanied them on the same wavelength syntony as the mother assumed on the maternity of these children. We can also say that there were no cracks in the marriage, since the marital agreement remained intact even with two young children. They continued working, relating to each other through their professional activities, and leaving these two young children in a sea of loneliness, despite the parents having no awareness of this.

We are going to imagine that our individual lets some time go by before requesting the next consultation. We will receive her with the images we shared previously, a beautiful queen looking out from the top of her marvelous mountain. Our protagonist wants to approach a subject that worries her: both children are poorly behaved at school, both have psychotherapists, psychologists, and speech therapists. They are thinking about adding a play specialist. They had tried punishments, taking away a vacation the children were wishing for, to no avail.

Since it has been six months since the last meeting, we will need to ascertain to what degree of consciousness - or rapprochement to her shadow- did our individual maintain during the time we did not see her. First, she talks about daily events, and soon begins to cry saying that she can't take it anymore and that she knows that something needs to change. We are on our way. Not to bore my readers, I will say that we will concentrate on reviewing the children's lives, from their birth until the present, from their own points of view. We recognize the loneliness, the displaced requests within this story, in relationship to a larger request for maternal presence, more availability, more play, and quieter moments. We will examine the tools these children have utilized to be heard, illnesses, accidents, fights, dangerous mischief, bad behavior, then worse behavior, hurting each other, threats to themselves, threats to other children at school, steeling, mistreating other children, disobeying. These are the few possible options that children have to express: "I am here, and I want you to be with me".

We will place each event in the chronological age of each child. We will confirm that these children want only one thing: that mom looks at them. Of course, from the mother's point of view, she feels that she lives for them, she works for them, and she strives to give them the best possible life. But these children suffer. They do not want what they have. They only want to stay in mom and dad's bed.

A global vision

By now, we have a global picture. For the first time, our heroine, can step into her children's shoes, she understands them and feels compassion for them. Then she asks the million-dollar question: What do I do? To which we will respond: "What you consider best". Knowing that each is responsible for his own decisions — we begin to draw a path that will help us integrate our shadow. Our individual, once she understands her character (which has been her best refuge), her need to remain hidden there, the danger of stepping outside her belief system, the challenges that lie ahead, her children's, her husband's, her employees', her enemies' (if she has any) points of view, then she will decide whether she wants to move the next token on the board or not. This is a personal decision, and it is none of our business as HBrs. In any event, if she decides to take a chance and move a piece on the board, we will be delighted to accompany her.

Now we have a few options. Is it this easy? Do we

build a **human biography** and then we can take steps that will bring us more happiness? No. This is an imaginary tale, very simple and without cracks. The real stories are much more complex. In any event, we cannot approach any issue until we know what character the individual is playing, without first being clear about the discourse of the "deceived I", without understating who is really talking, how afraid is she when stepping out of the refuge that upholds her identity, the character's advantages, and disadvantages, and of course, without first being certain of the individual's intellectual capability. When I speak of "intellectual capability" I want to clarify that some individuals have been highly mistreated during their childhood, even physically and emotionally abused, they often adopt the character of the one who does not know anything, does not understand anything and does not find out about anything. In all cases, the character is the costume that allows us to survive. If our survival hinges on not knowing anything, not perceiving anything, not registering anything…, this impulse takes hold to such degree that we can begin to function as "idiots". It is far from the mind not being capable; it is the soul that forced the mind to behave as an idiot, so that it will not bear witness to the atrocities -he already knows- he will not tolerate. It is not impossible to attempt working with the **human biography** in these cases, however we will need to pay attention and detect if this individual's inner being, could trust just enough to crack an opening in the idiot's costume who lives in the clouds and allow us to enter the dark corners of his shadow.

Everything is possible and sometimes nothing is possible. This methodology requires training, art, empathy and life experience. It does not fit everybody.

Fundamentally, we work on an ongoing basis to unmask the "deceived I" of those who consult with us, and never allow the clients to believe that the professional "knows" or is a "genius" or what have you. It must be crystal clear that this is an investigation worked in cooperation between two people: One is suffering and wants to know himself better; the other is not involved in the composition of the familial scene and will help by looking at the scenario from the outside. To achieve this goal, he will bring all the other voices, and be attentive to avoid entering the individual's scenario. If we offer an opinion, we are stepping into the scenario. If we feel anguished, or horrified, also. Thus, it is imperative to have listened to countless stories, and to constantly delve into our own shadow, so that our own character does not slip into the work we are doing on someone else's field. We must become a medium that allows, asks questions, organizes, and nothing more, nothing less. There is no room for our personal opinions, our philosophical theories, our beliefs or morals. This is "the other's" field. In this function we are a channel available to another individual's personal search.

Is forcefulness helpful?

What happens if a client feels what we are saying is too "hard"? This is a common fantasy. Nobody can say something that is "harder" or more painful than what the individual is already experiencing inside, whether he knows it or not. This is not the case of shooting interpretations at close range, rather than to name all that has not been named until now. If it truly "fits" with the individual's internal experience, he will simply confirm "that" which he has felt all his life can be "said" in words like those used by the HBr. If it does not "fit", then he will say no, that he does not feel like this. Nothing is lost. It means that we are mistaken, and we need to guide the investigation in a different direction. It is a detective's job. It is ungrateful. Because we often uncover realities that are much more hostile, violent, inhumane or fierce than we imagined. To search for the shadow is always painful; to remain blind is more painful yet.

What happens if the person who begins his process of **human biography** decides to change many aspects of his life, but finds that his spouse is not willing to change anything? Isn't it better to travel this path together? No. This is a frequent request from women. The women drag their partners to attend, listen and understand and tell us that we are right. Let's be clear that the proposal to integrate our shadow does not search for agreement in favor of some and against another, to the contrary, it proposes mutual understanding of the reasons behind our characters, to be able to decide whether we want to set those characters aside and live our lives more connected with our internal truth.

When we expect our partner to come to the consultation, we continue to assume that "the other one must change". Nothing is further from the truth. In fact, those aspects we despise in the other -whether our partner, our parents, siblings, neighbors or in-laws- is simply a reflection of an aspect of our own shadow. If something is manifest -with happiness or sorrow- on the scene, it is because it is part of our own plot, even if we cannot perceive it. If the plot produces mostly suffering, we can always change ourselves, then the entire environment will modify. Like in the game of chess, when a player moves a piece, the entire game changes.

Regarding the value of convincing our partner to start on this voyage: I only want to say that if the client -in case it is a woman- begins to perceive her own character, understands its benefits, admits the price others have to pay for her to maintain her role, accepts others' voices, looks at the entire picture and identifies what she triggers in others, perhaps she will be able to change. When she can change and relax, when she listens, when she stops fighting, when she can spontaneously address her partner with more care and affection...then the partner will be genuinely interested and will say: "I want to do this too!"

It strikes me how rare it is for men transiting the experience of constructing their own **human biography** to expect convincing their partners to join them. In general, there are fewer manipulator characters among men than among women, although this is only based on my institution's records, which could be debatable.

I can't find a more noble or generous approach than bluntly sharing with the client what we perceive in the picture. We have the duty to speak with clarity and simplicity. We are all intoxicated by confusions, deceits, lies, secrets, misrepresentations and foggy lenses; nothing could be healthier than firmness in our words that name true emotional states. This is not the case of interpretations. Here we attempt to name whole pictures and to verify to what extent they resonate with everyone's internal being. Why should we wait, go around in circles, mislead, disguise, soften up or manipulate the information? Indeed, this is what the adults did when we were children. This is what undermined our trust in our gut feelings. This is what took us away from our axis. A good detective, once he puts together the puzzle, and verifies that the pieces fit with precision, has the duty to share this vision with the owner of the **human biography**, the one to whom it belongs.

It surprises me that it appears "hard" to tell things "as they are" to an adult (for example, the emotional abandonment this adult experienced during his early childhood). On the other hand, we are not moved when we hide from a child the concrete realities she is experiencing in her own home, in front of her nose, among adults who are assuring her that what is really happening, is not really happening. This is maddening and cruel. It is never cruel to tell the truth. The truth may be hard, but by speaking it, it softens things up.

Certain characters fascinate us

There is a frequent obstacle for those who wish to train in accompanying individuals in their personal search, and that is the fascination produced by certain characters. The entrepreneur more than the depressive. The charismatic more than the quiet one. The spiritual more than the materialistic. However here is where we need to reach out for our own clarity. The individual who, through his character has obtained the admiration of the world around him…will be the most difficult to unmask. Because he is accustomed to receiving recognition for his work and thankfulness for his presence. Why would someone so captivating request a consultation?

For example, a shaman and meditation teacher attend the consultation. He is a charming individual, and he does not recognize any personal difficulty. Let's assume he is consulting because his wife is pregnant. He would like her to consider a more spiritual path and would like her to consult a naturopath, who is also his friend. She does not want anything to do with this, she is scared, and does not

153

want to veer away from the most conventional physician. In fact, she is consulting with her mother's, aunts' and older sister's physician. Our client, very elevated and mystical, with an enviably beautiful and serene face, is coming for help. Truly, he wants to know how to help his wife.

Two things could be happening: the first that we fall under the spell of this spiritual being who is coming to consult with us, therefore increasing our self-esteem; we decide to listen to him, and we will probably agree with him. As I have said if we listen…we are not organizing a **human biography**.

In this case, our character -I mean the HBr's character- slid into someone else's field, the client's field. In barely a moment we lost our role of companion in search of the shadow. When our internal little bell lets us know that we have lost our purpose, another little bell upholds the excitement and tells us that we should not make such a big deal, this marvelous being came to ask a very simple question. How could we not agree and have a conversation about the marvels of naturopathic professionals that assist magnificent births. This fascination played a trick on us. This marvelous and enlightened being will go home very happy. And blind.

The second option is to offer him to construct his **human biography**. His? Would he stoop this low as to tell his intimacy to any run of the mill therapist who is much less spiritual than he is? Perhaps he will be offended. He has the right to be. We can always explain to him that his wife is his, not ours. He chose her, he loves her, he shares his life with her, he got her pregnant, he is expecting a child with her and perhaps, she embodies that aspect of fear or rigidity he does not accept as his own. This easy. Something has to do with him, his shadow, his projections, his fears manifested in his wife's conventional choices. We propose that we inquire together, because perhaps, there is no need to change doctor. Perhaps, he needs to assume the share of rigidity that belongs to him, and then perhaps his wife will feel freer. We do not know, but we can investigate. If he understands that he is part of the plot and something about the scenario makes him uncomfortable, we could share the experience of organizing his **human biography** with the same warmth, intention, ability and affection as we do with everyone else.

Is it possible to accompany in the construction of a **human biography** with an individual we admire? To the extent that we detect that we have fallen in the fascination, and we are able to distance ourselves of our personal involvement. If we are not able to do it, it is better to refer the individual to a colleague. It is not impossible, but we need to understand what happens to us and be able to look at this individual like we look at any other. If we approach this work searching for the shadow with honesty and love, it is possible that we may admire this individual even more because of his commitment, dedication, humility and goodness. It would have been a pleasure to work with a true sage.

The images at the service of the human biographies

In my desire to stop paying attention at the interpretations and so many spoken words that go around when we talk about emotions, I have been experimenting - in the beginning with outlines: lines, dots, arrows, or circles, and later introducing images- until I found a synthesis that would allow a better understanding among professionals and clients. I realized that often each person would provide a different meaning to each idea. What does it mean that someone loves me, that he is kind to me, or I am affectionate with her, that someone is unfair or that I am good, that someone hurt me, that I am right or that the world is cruel? These are subjective conclusions which do not mean the same to everyone. On the other hand, in these times of audiovisual culture and little patience to read explanations, I have attempted to show the complete scenarios through images. It is showing good results. The human behavior is very complex; however, it appears that we have been able to capture the concepts in 140 characters or in a 14 second audio. As you will see, I try to adapt to our current times, and I verify that the use of images works.

At which stage of the process of the **human biography** are we able to offer the client images? At any time. We often propose an image that encapsulates the childhood subjective experiences -once we have established in broad strokes what happened when the client was a child- and then we will offer a second image that represents the individual's survival mechanism, the character that offered protection. Throughout our path, we will typically use **two images**: the first representing the childhood scene and the second representing the character that helped us survive this environment. Obviously, the scene and the character have much in common.

We have said that at the beginning of the **human biography** we will deal with the childhood. In general, will observe much more lack and sadness than the individual remembers. For example, we could show the image of a desert. A child alone. A frightened child. Or perhaps the image of a gigantic mother occupying the entire field without considering any children -even if there were five children-. An image of fights and drunkenness among adults, without any children in sight. An image of perfection that mom and dad demanded, using the image of a line of unmovable stick soldiers. These are images that transmit an emotional reality and allow the client to identify. Of course, the HBr will search for an image that coincides with the tales, and most especially with what the individual cannot verbalize, because he does not know it, but the professional intuits. This places us within an agreement. What are we talking about? Of the emotional desert and the lack of affection, warmth, softness. We start from a basic agreement. The childhood was a desertic place. If the HBr and the client are in sync, we can draw some hypotheses: perhaps some cacti will be able to grow here, but there won't be any exuberant tropical vegetation. To do our detective work, it is imperative to have some logic.

Childhoods are not terribly different from each other. We swing between pure loneliness to the most explicit violence. There will be an abundance of lonely children, or adults occupying the entire field. Perhaps more war, more abuse, more aggression or more alcohol.

The true challenge will be to listen to this individual while we are imagining what was this child doing, later as adolescent and young adult, to survive. How did he "arm" himself to survive this family war. This character, this plot, this mechanism…this is what we will try to identify with one image. This will be the image that will concern us for the rest of the **human biography**, not only it helps the hero of the story to save himself, but it will also establish a scenario where the other actors will have to situate themselves by obeying certain rules. The rules that the "game" requires.

I suggest a "recess" to train the mind. I will offer a few images, belonging to little stories that fit the image, so that we can see how people who are emotionally close to us, feel when we own this image.

Until now the HBrs in my group have drafted their own drawings. Sometimes they have searched images on Google and have printed them. I have asked the talented graphic artist Paz Marí to help with this book, as she has been able to interpret the feelings I am trying to convey through the images; she has drawn the images inspired by the spirit of the tarot cards. Perhaps sometime in the future we will have a few dozen cards available to the professionals engaged in the **human biography** methodology.

Here goes the first one: **Pride, the proud one.**

Pride, the proud one

We use these images when we conclude that our client got himself comfortable atop a mountain, looking at the horizon, finding refuge in his mind and greatly valuing his intellect.

This emphasis was likely present since childhood and may have been a merit to be reached, valued by the mother. The issue is that this child will attempt to be loved by showing his value, until obtaining acknowledgement and feeling safe on a top rung. He may despise those who are not like him and exercises his pride or mistreatment towards others. He obtains several benefits: he likely has admirers in some area or other, people who praise and fear him. These can be his partner, his children -if he has them- or his colleagues at work or at school.

Finding refuge at the top gives us a sense of security, primarily because it allows us to be in control. To dominate gives us relief. The benefit of this character is the power of command, with value on intelligence; we capture a place of superiority and respect from others. Let's look at some of the disadvantages. It jumps at you: loneliness. There are no peers. No one is at our level. We complain that no one helps us. How could they help us? It appears that we don't need anything. "To need something" is what happens to less valuable people that are down there in the swamps of the commoners. There are other disadvantages: with so much isolation and so much intellect…there is little emotion left. The heart is not beating. It appears there is no blood. If there is no blood, there is no sex. The mountain air is like that: pure and clean.

Likely the HBrs will propose this image when we are talking about the client's youth. By then, we would have listened to multiple opinions in favor of intelligence, or we have detected scenes where **our client** was elected by a professor because he was "brilliant". We do not judge whether one thing is better than another. We just observe the logic. If an individual finds refuge in the purity of reason, when it is time to build a partnership, he will select one of two options: the first is to have a relationship with someone as mental as himself or herself, with whom he will get along fine, will share the same likes and activities, some common goals and possibly limited sexual passion. The second is to have a relationship with someone who approximates the "opposite": a sensible man or woman, connected with their internal world. Simple. Perhaps connected with the earth or the arts.

During the courtship it will be a sure thing because a softer individual brings the subtle world to the intelligent one. Years later, if she is a female, has children and perhaps a financial difficulty, she will demand of her partner to take on a professional career, to have a clear objective and to earn money. No one is saying what each partner must do. We are only looking at what one character in his/her scenario is proposing to the other actors. If the brilliant and proud woman who is observing the world from the top of the mountain suffers…perhaps the first smart response would be to slowly climb down this magnificent mountain to see what we are able to see. This is what an image can offer when we are metaphorically working with her, instead of getting caught in interpretations about what one says, the other betrays, and how unjust the world is.

Let's continue working with this new image: **The male fighter. The female fighter.**

The Fighter

A male or female armored warrior. We appear brave. We are ready to do what it takes to win our battles. It is very likely that our childhood was dangerous (in fact, it is possible that we have outlined our childhood scene as a war image, all against all), therefore we learn since young to defend ourselves first and attack next. We only feel safe when we are wearing our armor. What are the advantages? We can win any contest, go through conflicts, fight for what we believe is right and win. Yes, we will win. We know how to win. We have enough fire to confront anything. Here there is good sex. Blood and passion. Adrenaline and vitality. These are advantages we don't want to lose once we have tasted the flavor of victory and strong emotions.

What are the disadvantages? What happens to those in relationship to the warrior? It depends whether we are enemy or ally. There are no other options in this scenario. There are no indifferent actors. There are enemies as powerful and fearsome as the protagonist, or allies, not necessarily as powerful, but need to follow orders and will allow the protagonist space and freedom of movement. It is possible that our partner will be someone quiet, without much desire of his/her own who allows us to carry him away by the wake of our force and energy. If we do not change the rules of the game and we maintain control, there won't be any crisis. The problems show up if we are women and gave birth to children, if we need to soften and we expect someone else will take on the warrior role, if we are wounded or sick. Someday this will happen. At that time, we will have to observe how much we value our gumption and vitality at the service of our fights.

Let us think about another image: **The Wall**

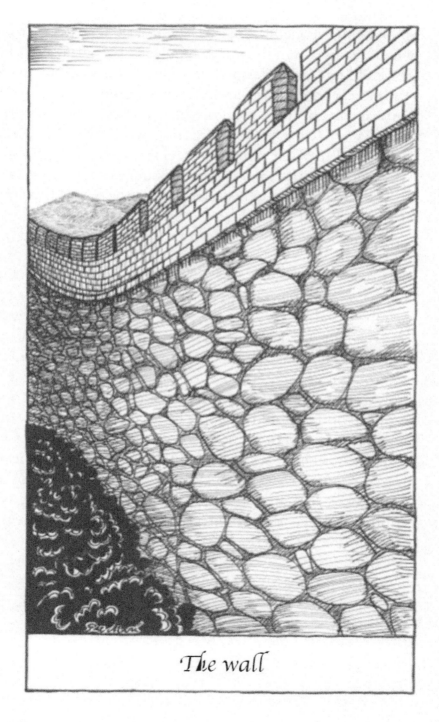

The wall

If we conclude that a client will feel understood when we show him the image of a wall, it is because during his childhood, he decided to seclude himself to avoid suffering. We go inside and we are shut up. It is probable that we have been subject to violence and abuse inside the home, we have concluded that the world is a dangerous forest, and the best option is to close ourselves up inside. We build great internal walls remaining prisoners but safe. Later, this confinement created a reserved, hard, distant and suspicious personality.

Advantages? We feel protected and accustomed not to interchange with anyone. To the extent that the environment remains the same, our sense of safety increases. Nothing unexpected, nothing out of place. No surprises. Stability is very necessary for the child's universe. Later, when we become adults, we need to maintain our primary feelings within a framework of extreme stability.

Disadvantages? The world is narrow, we have few life experiences, few emotional relationships, and we only establish bonds with the people closest to us. We marry our childhood friend or a neighbor. Our life is limited. Our goals are modest. We are afraid because we have never been outside our fortress walls. Life happens on the other side. Those in our circle will suffer our narrowness, our stubbornness, or our inability to think or dream outside the conventional or trite.

Let us look at another image: **The fairy tale**

The fairy tale

Here we are inside a children's tale. Of course, it is a fantasy from beginning to end. We have remained childlike, believing or inventing stories to avoid suffering. If life has been hard, here we did not get the message; anyway, we are inside a tale running through a field of flowers. We have left for Neverland. Let others take care of the mundane problems. This is not too bad a refuge, because we are "happy". We tell our own tales, interpreting the events from a fantasy point of view.

It is possible, the more we insist on our field of flowers, the more we are "disillusioned" or "someone betrays us". If we observe what generates this image, there are relatives to whom something happens, they ask for our help, despair...but they always encounter our obstinate happiness.

I want to point out, those of us who decide to live in our own tale, elicit a burst of fury from everyone else. Not only because it is impossible to establish a relationship with someone enclosed in a fantasy, but also because we won't be interested in anything else that does not fit with the fantasy we built in our heads. In other words: no real person exists in the protagonist's fantasy tale. This is a very difficult scenario for everyone else. Not so for the owner of the image. It is fantastic. In these cases, it will be difficult to consider change, since nobody wants to lose the benefits of the illusion that holds us in a constant state of happiness.

Another idea: **The wild horse**

The wild horse

A runaway horse. Desperate. Crazy. He marches on without looking nor thinking about his destiny. A wild horse, as soon as freed from his rope, will run anywhere. We have been brutally wounded; thus, we escape. This is what we have learnt, and this is what we do.

Our ability to run away -same as with other characters we have adopted- has allowed us to survive. What happens is that we are trained to continue doing "this" automatically.

An individual who runs desperately, without allowing himself to stop, think, evaluate or discern, will miss some good opportunities. The engine is the permanent fear and the imperative need to run away.

What happens with those we are in relationship with us? You won't register them. There is rarely someone else on the scenario. It is noteworthy that we are often dealing with a mother of three, the head of the family or someone responsible for the wellbeing of others.

The emotional closeness burns, because when we were children, we had painful experiences with contacts that have hurt us. Thus, we live in constant flight. During these frightened races, we have little awareness of our environment, and we minimize the hurt we inflict on others.

Let us observe a common image to illustrate our childhood, which often continues to have validity during our adulthood: **The desert**.

We use this image to provide a graphic form to our childhood experience. We learned to live in utmost austerity. I am referring to the emotions, not the finances, although sometimes the austerity filters to all areas of life. We can manage with the minimum required to survive.

The desert

We are surrounded by dryness, rudeness, stone, dust and thirst. We do not feel deserving of anything, and love is very far away and unattainable. When we were children, we got accustomed to crossing the desert, thus we conclude that we do not need anything nor anyone. Our needs are

minuscule, the suffering will be lesser, because we do not have any kind of longing. No one can frustrate us or hurt us. It is a good trick to feel free. There is nothing to desire beyond what is fair and necessary. We are not aware of the lack.

Little by little, we become acquainted with emotional abstinence until we reach significant levels of emotional indifference, preferring that our environment keeps a certain distance not to bother. If our partner, friends, children or relatives desire more water, more food, more hugs or more company, it will seem an exaggeration and disrespectful. What is the right amount? Each one of us tries to fit their own. We should know that when someone close to us is demanding more affection, more tenderness, more soft words, more warmth, more comfort or more rest, what matters is to be aware of our minimal needs compared to others' needs. An oasis may feel like an exaggeration if we have already quenched our thirst. For an individual living with the minimal expression of personal needs, an oasis serves for just enough. It is not meant for the enjoyment of luxury. However, we cannot imagine the torrent of love we hold inside if we ever allow ourselves to melt away this false harshness.

Observing another image: **Proximity to danger**

Proximity to danger

The embodiment of danger. We know that something or someone is lurking nearby. We feel his breath behind our back. We can never sleep peacefully. Society tends to dismiss the paranoiacs' disturbing sensations. However, for those who suffer, the real internal experience is of clear and present danger.

Evidently, when we were children, the predator was our mother. If the one who was supposed to care for us, was the one who most assaulted our physical and emotional integrity, it is to be expected that the world will be a dangerous place.

When we come from a dangerous scenario, we live between extreme alertness and a paralyzing fear, swinging between both sensations, between power and helplessness.

Often, we feel alone and misunderstood, because we do not know how to share or communicate the level of permanent distress and the feeling of impending death that accompanies us every moment of our lives, even if there is nothing "real" attacking us. However, the predation existed and was terribly real for the psyche of the child we have been.

Later, as adults, this is how we will relate to others. We mistrust, we are unable to surrender to love and our relationships tend to be transactional.

We associate life with control. There is no trust, pleasure, surrender, or fun. Only danger.

Another image: **The kite**

The kite

Free like the wind. Light. We go where the breeze takes us. Without direction nor desire, objective nor goals. It can be fun for a while, even if we do not have consistency. A puff of air and we disappear. We accommodate to anyone's desires, perhaps we later complain that we are not happy with the destination where we landed.

Sometimes "talkative" individual tends to adopt this character, we like the plays on words, and in the end, we do not convey any solid or coherent meaning. We confound our listeners since we can "turn around" any event using colorful interpretations.

Advantages? Freedom. We do not search for security. We do not hang on. We can change direction without much drama. We love the future and the uncertainty.

Disadvantages? Our relatives feel responsible for us, since we are flying around from here to there. Those of us embodying this character are not responsible for ourselves or anyone else. Here today, there tomorrow. We force others to take control and define the direction, while we fit into any travel route. If something goes wrong, it is not our problem, since it was someone else's decision. We come from scenarios with scarce affective roots, we have been abandoned long ago and we decided to keep walking without looking back.

Here I share an image that we use with great frequency: **The wolf in sheep's clothes.**

The wolf in sheep's clothes

The HBrs have a hard time detecting the character of the wolf in sheep's clothes, as deceit is this character's primary vice. Of course, at the beginning of the investigation, the professionals can be deceived too! Especially when the characters present ourselves as victims, telling us in detail the hardships caused by some horrible person that makes us suffer: our partner, our employer, our boss or our ex-sister-in-law.

It is likely that our mother taught us how to lie or disguise, having been witness of her machinations she used to satisfy her own needs. In other cases, we have developed our own cunning because of lack of care, affection, and emotional availability from those who raised us.

The HBrs -as detectives- we need to have sharper ears than the wolf's, precisely to detect his melody. Only the sum of all the events can provide a clue. The wolves have learned to pass undetected; we have trained to establish alliances and the art of obtaining our objectives without anyone noticing. We count with many naïve allies. It is a difficult character to let go, because we have an insatiable hunger and we have learned to satisfy our needs. The wolves in sheep's clothes win almost all the battles, because we can snatch the best morsel without anyone noticing.

Finally, I share with you the image of: **The little closed package**

The little closed package

If we establish our character withing a small box tied with a pretty bow, it is because we have suffered too much, and we are not willing to let anyone inside our internal world. Occasionally, our childhood scenario was narrow and repressed, administered by our mother's fears that imprisoned us in an environment so tiny that we have lost all reference outside our familiar environment. We settle between our four walls. Within this system we cannot offer anything to anyone either. We have so much fear that we do not open, offer nor exchange anything at all in any area of our life. We tend to organize our routines based on obsolete prejudices, pre-established and fixed ideas, to the extent that our thoughts shrink to fit within a few cubic inches. A little package we are unwilling to open. Life develops inside there. There is very little room. We do not care. Let each person close himself up in his own little package and do not bother us.

I share with my readers these images as a sample. The intention is to train ourselves to observe how each scenario "forces" certain movements, so that we can continue to live within the logic of the plot, instead of the logic that everyone else proclaims. As I have explained many times, what we say doesn't matter. The discourse is deceived. The facts and events are the truth.

To clarify, I will offer a few life stories and their respective images. We will likely identify with some more than with others, but in any case, it will remind us of someone we know, we love or despise. That means, they belong to our plot. I hope the stories are useful.

The tornado

Marcela traveled to Buenos Aires to attend her first consultation -she did not want to meet via a virtual videoconference-. She lived in a mid-size town in Patagonia, she was fifty-six years old and had two adopted daughters, Marilina and Estefania, eleven and twelve years old. She was in the middle of a divorce. She had attended psychoanalysis sessions for over 20 years. When she read my book *El poder del discurso materno,* she was moved and decided to try this system. Marcela wanted to know why she was so violent with her daughters, especially because she knew it was bad, she could not "stop herself". She said this crying, visibly sorry.

We offered to start her **human biography**, beginning with her childhood experiences.

Her maternal and paternal families were from middle class extraction. Her parents married when they were very young. Marcela was the oldest of four children. She was named as the most intelligent and kind. They lived comfortably, and although there was money available, the father was very miserly. Who said this? I have mentioned earlier that the memories are organized based on the discourse of who has named reality. In order to reach the child's reality, we need to look through the lens of who is looking at this life history.

At first, it seems easy to figure out that it was the maternal discourse. Mom did not have access to money in the manner she wished. The verbal violence between mom and dad was a daily occurrence. The mother would hit the children often. The father less often, but when he did, it was brutal.

We ask about her schooling, moments of refuge, fights among siblings, any problem within the family (we tend to ask questions that will help us organize the memories and establish a probable panorama). In each case, Marcela remembered all her efforts to make sure her mother would not be crossed because of the work the younger brothers required. She could not remember herself playing; to the contrary, she would watch her siblings play in the patio. In fact, her mother would repeat: "Take care of your brothers". She said that she hardly ate, which would enrage her mother. But however much she tried, she could not eat, it was revolting.

During her elementary and high school, she attended a religious school. At the beginning of adolescence, she saw herself as thin and ugly. She wore glasses. She never dared going to a dance and being close to the boys made her panic. Crying, she now realized her mother never asked her what was going on with her. Her younger brothers would go out, have fun and go dancing. She would stay at home studying, however, when she finished school, she did not wish to pursue any specific vocation.

Until now, we see a common childhood and adolescence, a fair amount of violence and repression. She was also given the responsibility over her siblings, which she apparently assumed. At age 18, she had no life experience, no friends, no desires, and no goals. She studied French and taught high school.

What could happen in her emotional life? As detectives, we imagine little to nothing. She had very little training. We let her know and Marcela confessed that she had several platonic relationships. She told us in detail each of these invented stories based on a glance, a smile or a

The tornado

coincidence, basically fed by her fantasy. Now she understood that at the time she had been very afraid.

We show her the image of the desert to illustrate her childhood. We say goodbye. A couple of days later we see her again in person, since she had traveled to Buenos Aires specifically for the consultations, despite our suggestions that she learn to use the computer or the telephone to facilitate future long-distance meetings.

During the second meeting we continue the chronology. We look at the image of the desert again. She continued living with her parents and nothing else; when she was thirty-two years old, she met Horacio, who would later become her husband. They met at a family event. Marcela was teaching classes at several schools, lived with her parents and had little else to report. It is not that she liked Horacio that much, but her mother pushed her to get married so that she would not become an "old maid".

Horacio was a simple man. In answering the questions that the HBr asked, Marcela responded in reference to her husband with a devalued and pejorative attitude; he was lazy, he did not accept jobs that required additional effort, and was not ambitious. The question regarding her sexual beginnings was duty. True? Guess what Marcela responded: They have never had any problems in this area. Is this credible? No, we are detectives. We are not talking about problems necessarily; we are talking about ignorance. A woman who is virgin at thirty-two years of age, still living with her parents, without spreading her vitality and with long lived fears…, her sexual life is not going to be easy. We told her. First, she denied with difficulty, but then accepted crying that she did not like to talk about "that". She agreed that she never had a "sexual appetite" and that was a problem within the intimate relationship. He wanted sex and she wanted him to find a good job. Early on they had some friction and little by little the aggression between them intensified. She focused on her work; he deployed his interests in gatherings and card games with his friends. She complained that he was never home. He contended that she declined him and therefore he would go out. The dissatisfaction was mutual.

At this point, as detectives we have two possible tracks: Marcela would "continue repressing" her longings and dissatisfaction doing "the correct thing" so that her husband would not get upset, or she would unload her repressed fury in identification with her parents. We only need to ask which of the two systems she deployed. She responded immediately that her rage had no limits and that once she was on the verge of setting the house on fire while her husband was sleeping inside. Very well, we already have a hypothesis to our investigation. It is clear to us that the rage can lay latent...until it explodes. The investigator must discover the lit fuse before it explodes. We can now show her a possible mechanism of explosion, perhaps the image of a tornado that demolishes everything on its path.

Years later they decided to have children, but she could not get pregnant. When we asked her why she wanted to have a child, she did not have an answer. Partly they responded to a social mandate, and Horacio was requesting it. As usual, they did all kinds of studies, analysis, hormonal treatments. It seems funny to me, because the specialists rarely dare ask with a little bit of tact and care about the quality of the intimate encounters. Few people know that the orgasms are fertilizing. Even if it is evident, few of us realize that without loving encounters -and sexual obviously- it is very difficult to obtain a pregnancy (especially if we are more than twenty-five years old). This

185

law does not rule when we are very young; we get pregnant by mere looking at each other!

These infertility cases are obvious. At least they should be obvious to a detective. This couple attempted in-vitro fertilization. There were several but unsuccessful treatments. Despite the many questions we asked, Marcela did not want to review her memories from this period. We could imagine the weariness, the disagreement, and the frustration that kept increasing over the years. At age forty-one, Marcela refused to continue with the fertility treatments. Then they decided to adopt a child. We summarized the emotional reality in which she lived: the emotional aridity, the missed encounters, the ignorance and the rage, we completed the meeting and said goodbye.

It took her six months to ask for another appointment. Apparently, her psychologist discouraged her from continuing this line of search. Finally, she decided, she learned how to use the videoconference software and connected timely from her home. She said she was depressed, she had found out that Horacio had a girlfriend -to make matters worse, it was a woman she knew-and this hurt her very much. We told her that we preferred to continue with the chronology and pick up with the arrival of her daughters, and we would see later if the situation that had so overwhelmed her, was truly important.

The events surrounding the period when she wanted to adopt a child were very confused. We could not end up understanding who had the desire. First it was Horacio who wanted children, but she oversaw taking care of all the bureaucracy. She said this in a plaintive tone. However, this was their functioning since they became a couple, therefore we did not see anything out of the ordinary. When they finally went in front of the judge for the adoption, Marcela was forty-four years old and did not feel she had the strength to raise a child. The court awarded her a two-month-old girl. She saw her as infinitely beautiful and a few days later they took her home. The pediatrician recommended that she hold the baby in arms all day long, but something inside, very strong, would not allow her. We told her that we understood perfectly. The rigidity and the repression from where she came made it impossible to maintain the physical and intimate contact with her daughter. We spoke much about this, as it was the first time, she seemed to be able to "touch" the profound meaning of this "life-long disconnection".

How do we imagine she spent the baby's first months at home? If we are detectives and we observe the degree of emotional disconnectedness Marcela had experienced throughout her life, the disagreements with her husband and her general emotional ignorance…, we would know that the emotional intensity required by a baby would make her go crazy. We told her so with simple words, not to waste time with fancy words and misleading discourses.

Initially the baby was "very good". This is common with adopted children arriving at their new homes "used to" not making too many demands, because they have already experienced "lack of satisfaction of their most basic needs". We hope that at some point, the young child "realizes" that she has the right to demand better care. Personally, I believe this is a time to celebrate, because it means that the child begins to trust that if she requests, she will receive. While remembering those early months, Marcela realized that from the beginning she was more focused on her own rigidity than any intuition that could surface. Of course, they decided that the baby should sleep by herself in her own room, she removed the diapers as early as possible and closely followed the childrearing guidelines that perfectly fit her own childhood experience. A year later, they were notified that there was another baby girl available for adoption. Without thinking twice, they completed the documents and brought her home right away. They had a one-year-old toddler and a newborn; obviously there was total chaos in the household that neither Marcela nor Horacio could foresee.

They were immediately overwhelmed by the situation. Obviously, the repressed violence was unleashed. Marcela was reticent about providing details, therefore we, as detectives, provided words, because we do not care to judge, we care to understand the logic of a specific reality. This is a map of great rigidity, emotional ignorance, high repression of feelings, and scarce emotional resources. Two babies under the care of a couple without agreements and without true affection can only lead to an explosion. Therefore, we help by naming possible scenarios, until Marcela was able to accept and organize her mind and her heart.

Marcela would not stop crying. Both she and her husband had hit the girls with fury; they would yell at them, they would keep them enclosed in their rooms, they would threaten them. They could not love them. Both felt that the girls had ruined their lives. They felt it was unbearable to be at home as the girls' crying was unending.

We listen carefully, without judgement but attempting to expose the magnitude of the violence the girls have been subjected to, because only by tackling the magnitude of the emotional abandonment suffered by these babies, we would know what to do in the future. We ask her if she is aware of the degree of violence she has exerted over her daughters and she responded in the affirmative. In fact, she had asked for help from a group dealing with family violence, but soon after she suspended her consultations for fear that her children would be taken away, since her final adoption had not been completed. It is important for us to see the entire panorama, like a deck of cards that we spread and gather once and again; the rigidity and lack of affection from which she came was now being spread in the lack of affection toward her daughters. We understand the evidence of intergenerational chain of inability to love. It is logical and terrible. We needed to understand to be able to act in favor of those girls, who should never receive another beating.

Marcela understood but asked: How do I do it? I do not want to mistreat them, but I pull their hair, I scream at them, I insult them…it is very difficult to change. The HBr read her an excerpt from one of my books. "It is encouraging for a young child to hear his mother or father ask for forgiveness and committing to offer more care and attention." Marcela understood that we were suggesting speaking with her daughters about this subject and that they should not allow her any more mistreatment. She bid an emotional goodbye.

During the next meeting she felt sufficient trust to tell in more detail some of the atrocities to which she subjected her daughters. The professional was appalled and showed her again, through the computer screen, the force of the tornado's image, because it appeared that the children were left devastated after Marcela would cover each daily event with her overwhelming violence.

Marcela looked at the image and this time she exploded in tears: "Yes, this is me. Exactly like this. No one had described me so perfectly". She was crying because of the pain her mistreatment generated in her daughters. She knew she had been very harsh and unjust with them, that she had difficulty empathizing with childhood, but now she realized the gravity of the heartbreak. We told her she was also crying because of her own emotional abandonment, even as these words were not meant to justify her actions, but it was important that she understood what had happened when she was a girl and what price she had paid. Instead of becoming a loving and generous woman, she became a violent woman that razed her daughters' goodness to the ground. She recognized that at the time she adopted the children, she had held some intellectual arguments in favor of the adoption, but no emotional connection with her true internal emotional being. Several times we spoke about the past and the present, observing the logic of her scenery and openly displaying the true dimension of the cruelty, the fury and lack of lovingness.

Then she told us that the prior week she had allowed the two girls to sleep in her bed for the night. They had been requesting this for a long time, especially from the oldest one, but Marcela had never allowed them. A few minutes later she notices that Estefania was crying silently. Marcela felt paralyzed, she was unable to ask her what was happening to her, she was incapable to hug her, she did not know what she was supposed to do. Soon she perceived the ire that was growing inside. She felt her internal volcano, her tornado, her fury. At least she was able to be aware and was able to avoid hurting or threatening them. She breathed deeply and remained quiet.

We need to follow in detail Estefania's twelve years of life, and Marilina's eleven years of life. These girls had been shattered and we needed to "undo" the path with a new contemplative and compassionate look until we can "touch" each act of violence, each injustice, each aggression, each punishment.

We learned that Estefania had been medicated since she was three years old. Why? Marcela did not know exactly why. "She was nervous". She was medicated to "calm her down". We attempted to deal with specifically the moment in which they began medicating the child: if something specific had happened, if the child had been pressured - although we knew that aggression was common currency in the family-. The child was under so much that only a robot would not have been nervous under those circumstance. They had taken away her diapers although she did not have sphincter control yet and she was beaten every morning when she had wet her bed. The child had difficulty focusing on school; she did not write down what the teacher would write on the blackboard. We showed Marcela that it would be very difficult for a child to focus on school when there was such a degree of violence and disconnectedness in the household. Both Horacio and Marcela were very demanding with the studies, as the girl grew, she had less permission to go to her friends' homes or to participate in other activities, and more restricted at home she would be until her homework was completed. The same panorama. We asked her if she had ever asked Estefania about her thoughts, about what happened to her, what she desired. Silence. She had no idea. It never occurred to her to ask anything about her daughter. The medication -which Marcela did not know what it contained or what were the intended result- replaced the dialog, the closeness, and the interest.

It was obvious that we had to start from the beginning: she had to talk with Estefania. It could not be delayed, and Marcela had to find the capacity to obtain an approach, by telling her about her own childhood, what things she was afraid of…and leave an opening to be able to ask Estefania what she wanted, what she liked or what she needed. This seemed impossible to Marcela. We observed together the image of the tornado and, effectively, from the inside of the experience of permanent tempest, it appeared impossible to put on the breaks. This "evidence" had a strong impact on her.

We could take all the time we needed to review her own childhood, but right now there were two children living their own childhoods, and it was necessary to simultaneously dismantle her tornado's violence.

The virtual monthly meetings with Marcela continued. Her "automatic" response was very powerful. She continued yelling, pulling the hair at her daughters…but the daughters began to dare to respond to her. The youngest said: "You are worse than a dinosaur". At another opportunity she would have received a beating for lacking respect; but this time Marcela did not hit her. She was able to tell her daughter that it pained her to be called thus, but she understood. She immediately closed herself up in her room to cry, instead of leaving her daughter crying. It is a way of reducing the tornado's viciousness.

She had some encounters with Horacio when he was able to tell her that he was afraid of her. Fear of her violent and demeaning attitude. She did not disavow him but was able to listen. Her ex-husband and daughters would call her: "monster", "authoritarian", "destructive", and "steamroller". Instead of disparaging these descriptive, we would arrange them on the table and observe the scenario in its entirety, just as it is. In fact, for the first time, she felt a tender feeling toward Horacio, noticing she had never felt like that toward anyone. "Tenderness" was not part of her emotional reality.

The daily life with her daughters was difficult. Her "automatic" was always on the ready. Thus, the meetings helped her to fully observe her panorama, to see her tornado in action and to evaluate her complete ignorance regarding anything related to emotional connections. Our hypothesis is drafted, and each time we welcomed her with the tornado's image in front of the computer camera.

With these "small changes" in which she attempted not to yell or beat her daughters, she felt the house was in chaos. We asked her for some examples and, truly, the girls were doing what all children their age would do. However, Marcela found herself in a situation she did not know how to control, on top of this, she never found a way to make her desires compatible with her daughters' desires. She had no idea how to do this without her violent and demolishing character. Once Marilina started yelling that she hated everybody and especially "him". "Who do you hate so much?" asked the mother. The child responded: "I hate God because he made me born, he mistreats me, and I can't stop suffering since I was born…" and began crying with much anguish. Marcela was able to approach her without touching her and was able to tell her that God does not mistreat her, instead, she had mistreated her as mother and in any case, she was responsible for her pain, because she did not know how to care for her in the way she deserved.

This is how the path developed: each anecdote, each event, each reclaim, each angering, each disagreement, we had to place it within the general context reviewing the automatic reaction -the acting tornado- and then checking it with a more global understanding. How long? Until Marcela could train herself in the art of observing -like a hologram- her past life and her current life, her own childhood and their daughters' childhoods, understanding the automatic and violent system she puts in motion unaware, until we can completely deactivate it. We know this is far from simple.

Danger is lurking

A man with a tired and pained look arrived at the consultation. Danilo was fifty years old, and he had an eighteen-year-old son. He said he had spent his life hiding the sexual abuse he had suffered as a child and since then he had become a fighter, a manipulator and abuser of others. He was unable to care for the people he loved most and considered himself to be a horrible person, unworthy of trust, a liar and a trickster.

The HBr told him with tenderness that there was probably someone who had proffered "those words". Partly it was not very credible -since these concepts are loaded with debatable prejudices- in any case we could afford ourselves the opportunity to research them together. Danilo had done some psychoanalysis from the time he was twenty-six until very recently. We asked him what he had understood during those long years in therapy, and he responded that his therapists have been like fathers and mothers to him. Meaning, as it often happens…he could not explain a single clear idea about himself, after so much dedication to so many therapies.

We began the process of the **human biography**. As it is our habit, we ask about his birth and the family environment: both the paternal and maternal families belonged to high society, they were landowners and maintained a rigid catholic morality. Danilo was the fifth of seven children. Both father and mother used physical punishments as an effective tool in the children's education. All the children received beatings and each reacted as they could: some left the country very young; some confronted

195

the parents and others became sick. Danilo was noted the worse devil of them all. Literally, the devil. The father beat him with a belt, but even then, he was unable to correct him.

We looked for a loving figure during his childhood, but the children were in the care of domestic workers who changed often, and none became an emotional refuge.

We described with simple words the emotional abandonment bordering on cruelty, the enormous abandonment, the loneliness, the need to feel loved, which forced him to act out via desperate petitions to call his mother. Unfortunately, those cries loaded with pain were interpreted as "demonic". Danilo listened and agreed. He remembered that at the time he had panic of the dark and would sleep shaking with fear. He never knew why. Obviously, under the light of the panorama, it is easy to understand that he did not have other tools against the hostility and the hate.

We ask about his schooling, supposing as detectives that he had two options: pour his fury over his schoolmates or hide in front of the adversity. In his case, it manifested as a "devil". He fought violently with his schoolmates and as a result he would be expelled once and again from the school. As a result, he attended seven different schools. Danilo told several anecdotes describing his mischiefs - some truly dangerous- on our side, we noted to him that his mother was glaringly absent. Where was she? At home. What was she doing? We don't know. What did she say vis-à-vis Danilo's problematic behavior? That he was a damned child. Before saying goodbye, we shared with him that he appeared to have obeyed his father's moniker, endorsed by his mother; he was named as a devil and that is what he did: he fulfilled to the letter with the character he was given.

Our proposal would be to separate the character he was named from the real child, desperate for love since birth. We need to observe the scenario from the child's point of view with a clear gaze, to better understand his reality. He left with tears stuck in his throat.

During the following meeting new anecdotes related to his childhood came up; all loaded with repressed rage. There were scenes from the summers spent in the family's country home, filled with visitors, uncles and cousins. During one of those summers, a fourteen-year-old cousin began abusing him. He believes to have been six or seven years old when the abuse began, which lasted for a long time, although he could not tell us for how long. We talked about why the abuse continued and we concluded that it was the only environment of love during his childhood. We talked about the maternal delivery, the total lack of maternal care toward him and his basic needs, his need for care and protection and to have been a child left alone to his own devices. Even during the consultation, Danilo felt it was his fault to have maintained those secret meetings during his childhood, even when we showed him that the most painful aspect was the lack of love and the certainty that there was not a single adult around in whom he could trust and ask for help.

We believed it was incumbent to explain that the only responsible party were the adults, especially his mother who should have protected and loved him. An abandoned child is a child seeking love, and seeking love, sometimes he finds abuse. The abusing child was in the same situation as he was: impatiently looking for love through the submission of someone weaker. Talking of the devil, who is the devil here? The desperate children or the adults thrusting the children into the fire?

Obviously, in this environment he was unable to concentrate in school, which increased his father's ire and resulted in additional punishments. Danilo was unable to understand what was being taught in class and did not know how to find a solution. He went from school to school; he made friends with street urchins instead of forging friendships with the children in his school. He was initiated in the use of alcohol and other addictive substances. His father was a very distant person, his mother was submerged in alcohol and her own complaints. He remembers telling his mother that he was starting to take a lot of drugs, but his mother went to bed to sleep. We observed together this desolate panorama. We showed him the image of the "desert" to provide a graphic image of his childhood.

It was evident that he had been a lonely child and - without receiving any care – he suffered abuses; however, he had a certain capacity to understand he was in danger. Now we need to investigate what this child had to do to survive. As detectives, we have a couple of hypotheses: he could either learn to manipulate and steal something valuable from others, or he could be asleep with drugs and alcohol not to suffer too much.

We approach his adolescence with those two "suppositions" in hand. He started dating a lot of girls (we could say: "he consumed a lot of girls"). He had a strong sexual attraction for women, in fact he would have multiple relationships simultaneously. Of course, some women would leave him, and when this happened, he would go crazy, as if he could not tolerate the subtle connection with the feeling of "desert". In these cases, he would increase his alcohol consumption. These relationships were a constant in his life: he would have an intense relationship stemmed from his seductive capabilities and his masculine strength, but then he would subtly mistreat the women (and his friends and co-workers he would sooner or later antagonize).

He worked at some companies rising rapidly up the ranks and sharing adrenaline between the job and the passing relationships. In his blind race, he left the wounded by the wayside, consuming substances, affections, friendships, or circumstances that benefitted him. Later, these wounded would become his enemies, that means dangerous people who could hurt him. Suddenly he started crying unconsolably, as if some pieces were beginning to fit together in some of the stories of his relationships. We accompanied him for a while without rushing to calm him down.

He commented that he was anguished because he needed to earn more money. We asked in detail and found out that every time he finished an important relationship, he remained "committed" to continue financial support, partly to pay for the emotional damage he inflicted. He must be doing something "bad" for these women to be so mad at him and then childishly, he would find himself in the well-worn role of deserving punishment. At this moment it occurred to us to show him the image of danger.

We had glimpsed Danilo as coming from an emotional desert, yes. However, he was always constantly stalked by an imminent danger. He felt he was using too much energy to distract the "monster" so that it would not devour him. We told him that we suspected he was experiencing his emotional relationships with women as such, with his "automatic" mechanism: he would hurt them -in such a clumsy way we suspected it was unconsciously "on purpose" and then, he ended up accused of being guilty.

The desert

First, he discarded the idea...but then he started thinking about it. He tallied how many messes he had orchestrated without realizing before ending several romantic relationships. We suggested he let this idea rest for a while and to meet again in a few weeks to continue the chronology and organize some items that will fit the pieces of the puzzle.

At the next meeting we talked about the birth of his child Ariel. He was born of a six-year relationship. First, he wanted to tell us a rose-colored tale; that Ariel was a cute baby, that he had brought joy to their lives, and he had found happiness. From our point of view of detectives, and observing Danilo with his adrenaline to the roof, this was hardly believable.

I insist that to us it is of little to no importance what the client is telling. Once we have an image as hypothesis, we look at our own clues instead of listening. Until now we have a desert that hurts and an imminent danger that propels him to act. We do not see a shred of happiness in this scenario. We told him. The reality is that he would leave every day to go to work and when he returned, he would find his wife in a tizzy. Now he recognizes, remembering during those times he would get into a relationship as entertainment. His partner was a younger woman, and she felt the baby was her jailer. All she wanted was to return to her previous life. However, she was caught with this baby at home and a husband who was disconnected from anything that was truly happening.

We attempted to ask more specifically about this child's experiences, but Danilo could not remember anything, or at best he had a very superficial view about his child's first years. Unwillingly Danilo accepted that when he was at home, he was very intolerant with Ariel, although he did not allow the mother to hit him, because she was "very nervous". Here is our detective coming to intervene. Let's look at this: we have a man filled with work preoccupations, excitement, alcohol and fun loving; he also has a young partner, lacking experience and nervous, at home with a baby she does not tolerate. What is going to happen? Everything and anything. Why is he not saying it? Because he does not know it: he was out of the house all day long. We show Danilo that he was not aware his baby must have suffered punishments, harassment, and rejection from his mother. Then, with pain, moving his head from one side to the other, agreed. He remembered during elementary school, Ariel had difficulty focusing and this irritated Danilo to no end. Although the coincidence between the father's childhood and the son's childhood was evident now...it was not obvious in the past.

Danilo began to "thread" his anecdotes until he was able to accept that his son had experienced similar situations to his own. Ariel maintained a prudent distance from his father and from his mother. Danilo complained that Ariel was "hermetic" and "had a sour disposition". However, by looking at the panorama in its entirety, now he was able to understand that perhaps Ariel no longer expected to find love or affection in either parent.

In any event, we were able to clarify that Ariel's emotional balance depended on what his mother was able or not able to provide for him. In the case of male clients, we do not review the lives of the children in that much detail, however we look at the lack of capability these men have deployed in the support, to facilitate and love the woman, so that she could offer a better quality of mothering to the children. Of course, the men need to understand the emotional reality of their children, to be able to compensate them now.

We continued with the chronology of the events. With a child at home, the marriage fell apart very quickly. Danilo did not want to leave the house "not to abandon his child". Here the detective interrupts to say: "This is not true". Basically, it is not true. If we look at the entire picture, we will know that Danilo did not want to leave the home because he was terrified of the desert. In the meantime, the war between the partners was ferocious and Ariel was always the witness.

It was clear that the loneliness was approaching as a knife thrust into his back. We looked again at the image of the desert and the image of imminent danger that stalked him. Once more we used simple words to express: "In your internal desert you were always alone and there was an imminent danger, a monster about to devour you. This has happened since you were a child. You searched for strategies not to fall into his claw; sometimes you escaped, other times you hid, others you filled yourself with noise and entertainment, others you consumed substances and some you crouched in fear. Now you are an adult, and you know that the monsters do not exist. However, your character continues to search for strategies and continues to operate as if." He closed his eyes and said that what the HBr described appeared to be the summary of his life and he needed a bit of time to integrate the images. He said goodbye and left.

During the following meeting, the work was always done with the image at hand, searching between the client and the HBr the logic of the scenario. It was difficult for him to understand that the monster was not outside, that he created the monster from inside. We proposed to continue narrating the scenes from his daily life. He had

Proximity to danger

relationships with several women until he joined with his current partner, Susana. A year ago, he had asked her that they move together. She had three children and lived next door to her ex-husband. Susana did not want to jeopardize the financial support she was receiving from her ex-husband, and she was afraid to lose. Danilo experienced this as a terrible betrayal. He could not believe that Susana "would do this to him". We had to show him this was not a betrayal, but a free decision from Susana, since she had never promised him anything different. However, Danilo was obfuscated and furious, putting forward all the reasons why he and Susana had to live together.

The HBr told him: "Truly, you have been betrayed, a woman betrayed you. It was your mother who betrayed you when you were a child, and you deserved her protection". Danilo raised his eyes with rage and yelled: "I know that already!" and began sobbing as a child. Then we came back to the painful images from childhood, but this time adding the concept of betrayal once and again in detail, in each anecdote, in each hope and each disillusionment. Danilo was even more upset. Each time he had a disagreement with Susana, he would go out with several women at the same time, like a child seeking revenge. Of course, among those women he was left with a platoon of possible monsters: hurt women, wounded women, that made him pay the price for his impudence and deceived seduction.

We told him more less with those words, then Danilo confessed: "There is something I have not told you". About a year ago, in the middle of one of these infantile tantrums he deployed when Susana did not satisfy him, he left two women pregnant a month apart. One had an abortion and told him. The other held onto her pregnancy, accused Danilo of all the ills in the world and demanded that he acknowledge paternity. Danilo had just accomplished a new and flagrant "mischief" -if we can call it thus- with the consequent monster who would punish him for ever more. The baby had already been born, even if nobody in his environment knew of his existence: therefore, Danilo lived in fear of the baby's mother threats. This confirmed once more, his scenario beating to its own rhythm. We looked at him again. Danilo understood perfectly with his mind, but his heart was still overwhelmed with pain.

How can we continue? We had a complete panorama, but to live daily with his adolescent son, as choleric as him, with money problems and many debts, a demanding ex-wife, a partner he wanted but could not obtain, several women chasing him and a baby born outside of the official couple…it was overwhelming. However, we could accompany him for as long as he thought was appropriate, with the intention of taking apart each scene: to observe how they began, how he fed them, how he looked partly at what he generated and how he could begin to calm down that lonely and desperate child who was still quivering inside. We also told him that a possible way to exit this scenario is to stop reclaiming what he had not received as a child -that is maternal support- and to learn to establish relationships as a peer with a woman. Or with a friend. A new attitude that could help him change his story.

He let several months go by and returned, having listened to the recordings of the prior meetings. He was able to recount with his own words some scenes from the past and other from the present, where he could clearly see the monster stalking him and the infantile terror that paralyzed him. He saw the many times when he created the monster and then "fed" him, keeping him alive and awake.

Why people do this? Because of our "automatic" response. We reproduce, without awareness, the known scenarios.

He told us some details about the controversial divorce he was still fighting with Ariel's mother, whom he clearly "fed" for the last many years so that she would continue responding with ferocity. Then he was able to prolong his own terror without making conscious decisions. Here I want to show that each life has an infinite number of obstacles to confront, but when we understand the scenario in which everyone is immersed, the script written by the character and the hidden benefits, we able to suggest trying different movements. This would somewhat approach the concept of freedom.

The warrior woman

Melina arrived with her six-month-old baby in a stroller. She had been undergoing a therapeutic treatment with a psychologist, but since the baby was born, it was not the same, she did not feel "understood" and wanted to try something else. She was restless because she had to return to work and did not know what arrangements to make for the care of her child. She appeared to be a harsh woman, strong, with her feet firmly planted on the ground. She had just turned thirty years old. We suggested to begin with her **human biography**.

Her parents came from low-income hardworking families. Melina is the oldest of three children. Initially she said she hardly had any memories from childhood, but as we began to name, scenes of active violence appeared spontaneously. She remembered her mother always upset and hitting her harshly. She related a scene that was still very fresh: her mother had hit her with a hot iron. She told with similar detachment about several events in the same vein. The environment at home was of permanent war: mom obsessed with cleanliness and complaining about dad, dissatisfied and blaming the three children for not having been able to advance in life. Mom took care of the children and the house.

When dad would come home in the evenings, he also beat the children, and very much. With belts, chairs, shoes or whatever was at hand. We showed her that the children were used as shields by mom. Melina looked surprised: she never considered this point of view. However, she understood the meaning, as she immediately remembered that, after beating the children, father would come home with flowers and gifts for mother, and they established a game of compensation among the adults. This is something that Melina could not understand as a child. Of course, over time, she became a great defender of mom. How do we know? Because we are detectives. Because, despite mom being atrocious, she would spend the entire day drilling into their heads how horrible dad was, that she was the victim, therefore when dad would beat them, and mom would deliver them, the only thing she spoke of were the beatings from dad, not the delivery from mom (nor the beatings from mom when dad was away).

During the day, she and her siblings attended public school. She was a good student and did not give her parents work. She would go unnoticed at school. However, at home, she was always on alert waiting for the next beating. We took time to observe this war scenario where the children end up unfailingly wounded. If we are detectives, we need to think about our protagonist survival options: will she try to get by unnoticed to avoid the bullets, or will she learn to defend herself first and later to attack. This is what we need to find out.

To this end we tackled the scenes from adolescence, investigating her emotional relationships: how did she approach them? Running away from the relationships or fighting? How can we know? By asking directly, explaining that we are evaluating these two options. Usually, if we ask without beating around the bush, the clients can respond with total assurance. Effectively, she named the fights against her father. Why did she fight? Basically, because she was defending mom. Alright, as detectives we are outlining the warrioress character. We show her an image of the warrioress.

She looked at it and started laughing with pride. We continue investigating. The relationship with her first boyfriend lasted three years sprinkled with the condiment of jealousy, scandalous scenes and fights. At age twenty-one, after a fierce fight with her father, she left the house. She held some jobs and for many years she rented a room where to live. She touched some of the more marginal parts of society, she learned to drink, smoke and something else. Her only "friends" were those related to the use of drugs. It had been some time since she had fights and distanced herself from her high school friends.

With firmness we show her the panorama of this young woman entering the world and trying to figure it out the hard way.

We gave words to the scenes we imagined, and at this point Melina began to cry. Moaning she related fights with her friends, never-ending fights. The years of her youth were spent trying to survive, moving from one job to another, which she usually left amid great conflicts, going in and out of casual relationships with men in the alcohol circuit, and living precariously in places lacking comfort, and more. We suspect that there was likely a high degree of promiscuity, since it was part of the picture. She painfully agreed.

We look again at the brave, intrepid warrioress, survivor of all the battles. We also try to imagine the pain and tiredness she hides under her pretty warrioress costume. Here we say goodbye.

The next meeting happened within a short time. She related some anecdotes about much suffering that she remembered in the last weeks -once confirmed the pulse of the character- we suggested to continue with the chronology.

The Fighter

At age twenty-eight she met Hernan, her current partner and father of her child. It was a casual encounter at a bar, they had sex and that was the end of it. Melina attempted to tell us a pretty story that it was love at first sight, that she was smitten by Hernan's green eyes and everything else we can say from a place of deception. As detectives, we look at the heartbreaking image of this warrioress searching for a moment's rest. We ask her directly if she had seen in Hernan some modicum of stability. What are we searching for with these questions? To confirm if the warrioress is trying to conquer some territory that will allow her to rest. Effectively, Hernan had his own home and a stable job. We do not judge whether this is good or bad. We do not know, and we do not care. We are only trying to help everyone to look at their own scenario with as much logic and conscience as possible.

Obviously, Hernan consumed and much. But he would "lose control" only during the weekends. During the week he worked hard. Almost right away Melina moved in with him. Initially Hernan resisted but eventually he allowed it, with some conditions. Among them, that during the week there could not be any alcohol in the house, she had to work, and his mother had the right to come into the house any time she wanted. Hernan's economic proposal was strict: each had to contribute half of the expenses. Melina did not have much room to maneuver, and therefore "accepted" the conditions. If we look at the image..., it is not hard to see that the war would soon be unleashed.

She became pregnant almost right away. She worked until the last day of the pregnancy. She stopped consuming during the pregnancy but started smoking since she gave birth. We can imagine, as detectives and before we can verify, what could have been her experience of childbirth.

Her emotional disconnection, her need to make a great effort in front of any adversity and the fear of her own softness held her away from any loving experience. We told her so. Effectively, she had blurred memories from the birth, the attention at the hospital, and the mistreatment she received. There are no loving agreements shared with Hernan, no emotional intimacy, nor honest conversations or mutual knowing each other. None of this appears within her scenario of warrioress.

The newborn was unable to latch onto her breast (we look again at the image of the warrioress, imagining how could a baby breach all that armor). The baby hardly cried and slept a lot. We asked how many cigarettes she was smoking now. She said "few", but we already know that this "few" lacks credibility. Every time she smoked, she had to leave the baby.

If we have a warrior woman who goes out to fight every other moment and generates enemies every which way to be able to confront them..., what is going to happen with her baby in arms? Either the baby will become the principal enemy and she will confront him, or she will abandon him because the baby becomes the obstacle to wage the worthwhile fights. This is what the detective thinks before asking the client. Why do we think this ahead? Because if we naively ask how the postpartum period was, she will probably come from the automatic "deceived discourse", that is the words someone said. As the official discourse from the collective unconscious refers to the babies with a plethora of terms like "happiness", "happy face", "I am the happiest mamma in the world", etc., it is essential we search for the reality. It is more expeditious to find the reality when we follow a trusted clue.

Then we ask Melina if she experienced her child as an obstacle that stopped her from being able to fight or saw him as someone, she had to take care of. Melina thought for a moment and said she did not know. We ask her what Hernan's answer to this question would be. She knew the answer right away. Hernan had told her that she treated him like if he were her enemy. She distrusted everything. There was something else: strikingly, when her maternity leave ended and she had to return to work, Hernan offered her to stay home committing to take care of all the expenses. This was a great relief, but somehow, she was on the warpath. It was interesting to observe that, even without an apparent motive, her warrioress character was on the alert, always. Here we said goodbye.

During the next meeting she was very emotional. She had decided to tell Hernan what she was discovering during her consultations: how she made enemies of all her relationships, including him., How her automatic response kept her on the alert. How she mistreated everyone without realizing. Hernan thanked her, but also asked her to deactivate her constant aggression, since she was so hurtful with her words.

This allowed her to better observe herself during her fury attacks: she noticed when they began, how often and under which circumstances. Being detectives, what are we going to surmise? Yes, the baby is also going to be the depository of her aggressions. Sooner or later, it was going to happen. The nature of the scenario demands it. It is important to know this ahead of time and to express it without judgement, because we all share a moral degree, and we consider that mistreating a baby is a bad thing. If it is bad, we will have the tendency to dismiss or minimize it. It is the job of the professional to spread those cards on the table. We are observing reality as it is, so that each can have the most direct access to her own truth. We ask what Hernan did and what did the baby do during her fury attacks. They would be quiet. The baby would be very aware of her mom's movements. Slowly Melina began accepting that she often screamed at the baby, especially during the nights when he would not sleep. Most times it was the father who would calm him so that he could sleep.

We have a clear panorama. It was lineal. I want to say, for a warrioress, to have a baby is like taking care of an alien. In such an uncomfortable situation, that the character is going to react. Anything else would be impossible.

It happened that a few months after the baby's birth someone gifted her some of my books. She read them voraciously becoming a "militant" of the "childrearing with attachment", the disposable eco diapers and healthy nutrition. All this can be very interesting. One thing is to be in favor of ecological diapers, and another is to establish a loving relationship with our own child (or anyone else). In fact, she was able to generate a good number of enemies among the mothers who were "not in agreement" with this ridiculous "attachment childrearing". We look again at her image of warrioress, and we laugh a little bit. Now it is a bit funny. We say goodbye.

She returned several months later having self-observed herself in many and diverse situations. She was prettier and visibly more emotional. She told about different events in which she saw herself as extremely demanding with Hernan, although he had many great changes since the birth of their child. Her husband was available, he was earning enough money, he could calm the child, sometimes he would give him a bath or take him for a walk, especially when she would explode. Hernan was much more committed than she would have imagined before the child's birth. Several times, she recognized her moments of disproportionate fury, even if Hernan appeared willing to wait for her, support and help her. Hernan assured her that he valued the enormous effort she was making to be a good mother despite her history. This she related within a touching crying, as if the fact that someone would look at her with goodness and compassion, would disarm her.

Melina had returned to the consultations because she felt that this "tuning" enabled her to remember with more clarity the paternal sexual abuses during her childhood. We listened without surprise, since the sexual abuse fit within the law of this scenario we had approached. Over several meetings we allowed the resurgence of memories become clearer each time. The most important fact was to identify the level of alertness and mistrust she had displayed to survive. She began to feel very sad. Sadness is a new feeling and usually not compatible with the warrioress. One at a time, she was able to relate those events to Hernan, with modesty and suspicion. Even now, the daily relationship with her son, who was now a year and a half, felt overwhelming, sometimes she could not control her fury, but at least she was aware of it.

What else could we offer to her? We had reviewed her scenario many times and her character in action. Melina assured us that she understood everything but continued to suffer. We attempted to talk specifically about the daily scenes in which she was violent against her child. We were able to identify that generally, it happened at the end of the day, when the tiredness would overwhelm her. We thought of different strategies so that she would not be so exhausted, as it was obvious, we needed to protect her child. We also noticed that the fury appeared when moments earlier there was an inkling of sadness. As if the fury was protecting her from having contact with her pain. Melina asked: How can I abandon the violence if it is the only way I had found to stem off my depression? We told her we did not know, but if she was willing, we could continue meeting with her for a little bit longer. Reviewing scene after scene, providing a different meaning to her childhood fears, helping her reposition herself as an adult and responsible for a young child, searching inside herself for the strength to love and loving more each day.

Devoured by mom

Maria Rosa appeared to be a likeable and communicative thirty-six-year-old woman, married with a four-year-old daughter. She was worried about her role of mother, because she did not know how to communicate with her daughter. She worked long hours and she assumed this prevented her from having a good relationship with the girl. We asked her directly if her daughter ever asked her to sleep in her bed at night and without hesitation, she responded yes that each night was a fight, but since "everybody" told her this is a very bad idea, she had never allowed it. With some humor, we asked her who is "everybody", since, as detectives we suspect that "everybody" was probably her mother. In fact, this was Maria Rosa's mother's indisputable opinion. She also told us that when she read my books, she realized that she did not have a life of her own. Everything was vetted by her mother, and by the way, this was her husband's principal complaint. With this information, we began the **human biography**.

Both her maternal and paternal families had been hardworking Spanish immigrants of relatively reduced means. Her parents had an older child and twelve years later Maria Rosa was born. Regarding her brother Francisco she said that during childhood he "manipulated" everyone with his illnesses and made her mother's life difficult. We showed her that she was too young to come about those conclusions and those words seemed traced from her maternal discourse. She insisted that "everybody" would say the same. More concretely, who were those "everybody"? "Mom…well…you are right, it was truly mom". With tenderness we explained to her that if that child fell ill repeatedly or if he "manipulated" to receive maternal care, he was only doing what he was able to do to fulfill what he needed as a child. Mom was the one judging this child as "manipulator". Maria Rosa was annoyed by this comment, as if she needed to agree with mom no matter what.

With this annoying brother, it is to be expected that maria Rosa would occupy a more comfortable role in the family: she was good, obedient and an exemplary student. She was aware of her mother's pride when she was honored at school. Here we point out to Maria Rosa the strong polarization (organized by the mother) between the siblings: each one attempts to capture the mother's gaze from the character they were given, Francisco getting sick and Maria Rosa satisfying her mother's needs. What is missing in the scenario, projecting into the future, is the inescapable confrontation between the siblings.

We were unable to find a lot of childhood memories, except the terrible fights between Francisco and his mother. By then Francisco was an adolescent. She did not remember any physical violence but a lot of verbal violence. After the confrontations, Maria Rosa would calm her mother by telling her she would never do anything to make her mad and that she would always care for her. The father was absent from the scene, despite the many questions we asked. What was evident is that Maria Rosa was dependent and identified with her mother's suffering, which according to the maternal discourse, was the result of the older brother's behavior. It was obvious that the mother had trapped and devoured her; she had used her as a shield, to be protected, sheltered, and cared for.

Then we showed her the image of a girl devoured (in this case to generate a stronger impact, instead of drawing the image of a woman, we decided to use a crocodile's mouth that is eating up a girl).

She said this was very shocking and that it had not been quite like this. We told her we would continue investigating and greeted her goodbye.

She returned with the desire to relate many anecdotes. We explained we needed to draw a general sketch to find "the magic thread" of her life story. Then we could tackle the details. We started with her adolescence. What could be expect as detectives? She was not going to do anything that would ruffle mom. That was her brother's job. Most likely she was going to have a quiet adolescence without any upheavals. We asked, and effectively her life was spent between her school and the local parish. Her brother had left the house and life had become quieter. She met her first boyfriend through the parish. We asked specifically, but it turns out they never had sexual relations. After more questioning, it came out that they were just good friends.

As I said earlier, during adolescence we will search for two channels where the essential being unfolds: sexuality and vocation.

I want to clarify that in the histories flooded by the maternal abuse (this is what this **human biography** is all about), we rarely find a defined vocation. Why? Because in this scenario, mom is the only one having wants and desires. There is no room for anyone else to have wants and desires. If this were to happen, mom will expel him from the map. This happened to the older brother, who was exiled from the emotional exchange within this family.

Devoured by mom

It is important, in our role of detectives to understand ahead of time that is rare for an adolescent who has suffered such emotional abuse, hanging on the mother's desires and at the ready to satisfy her, to have sufficient emotional strength to develop her own desires. The young woman lives in the kingdom of the maternal desires. In any event, it is always necessary to ask and confirm our clues.

In fact, Maria Rosa had attempted some professions but quickly abandoned them, despite being a good student throughout her school years. We try to understand why. Maria Rosa offered a reason but then she would contradict herself. This subject ended without resolution. Finally, Maria Rosa got upset with so many questions. She wanted to know "how to be a good mother" without having to review the histories from the past. We assured her that we could not answer to "that". We have no idea "how to be a good mother". What we proposed is to accompany her to take the wool from over her eyes and to be able to look at herself. She complained some but agreed with us, and we decided to continue.

When she was twenty-four, while working at a clothing retail store, she met Roby, the manager. He seemed to have clear goals in life: to work, earn money, buy a house and have a family. He seemed the ideal candidate. Most likely he would also be in Maria Rosa's mother's eyes. Roby's parents and her parents were ecstatic, and the wedding was arranged soon after. Dear readers, please note that in this tale there is nothing related to intimate emotions, a coming together or any genuine exchange. In fact, after she was married, she realized she did not have a say on anything. Everything they did, ate or purchased was selected by Roby.

At this point we present again the image of the girl eaten by the crocodile. If this is the character indeed, we can see more clearly the complacent girl so that mom would be satisfied, would likely look for a man whom she can satisfy and in whom she can delegate the responsibility of desire. We had to go back a few "steps" in the game of **human biography**.

During her childhood, everything she did was an offering to mom. Mom needed to feel "proud" and to the extent that this was important to mom, Maria Rosa would excel. In those cases, mom fed her own wellbeing. No one was looking at the real girl. Therefore, even if she had good grades in school or excelled at the activities at the parish, it was to feed her mother. However, her own emotions, her internal needs, and her feelings…were relegated to the shadow.

Standing within this scenario and profoundly ignorant of her own being, Maria Rosa would not be able to have intimacy with her husband. In fact, this is exactly what happened. Roby worked long hours and she did too. On top of this, their schedules did not coincide. The weekends were spent alternatively at her parents' house or his parents' house.

A year later, she began with "depressions" and a psychiatrist medicated her right away. Do you see how this works? We have a genuine feeling, and instead of finding out what is happening to us, we prefer that someone puts us to sleep, anesthetize us and free us from the responsibility to understand ourselves more. A year later, despite nothing having happened within the marriage, she left her husband and returned to her mother's house. There were no words, reproaches, demands, desires, agreements or longings. Their sexuality was not a place of agreement or disagreement. Nothing at all. We return to the image of the crocodile's mouth, thinking about the harm caused by the abuses and how we can suppress the slightest emergence of personal desire. We shared this thought with Maria Rosa, but she refused to see it.

She felt safe in her mother's house. She worked in peace, and slowly but surely, she abandoned the psychiatric medication. She told a few anecdotes that confirmed that the mother directed Maria Rosa's life, although she was an autonomous adult. Until now, this agreement between them was working. Truly, she was happy to return to her mother's house.

The thing is that Maria Rosa was dedicated to working and spending the weekends accompanying her mother. With the money she was saving she began building her own flat…, above her parents' house, of course. During a vacation by the sea, she shared with her parents, she met Mario, her current partner and father of her daughter. When they returned from vacation, Mario moved into Maria Rosa's home, which was nearly finished.

Mario was a traveling salesman. He would spend some periods of time away from home, while at other times he was engaged in administrative tasks and maintained a regular schedule. As detectives we assume that Maria Rosa did not need to or did not know how to have an intimate relationship. Because her flame of vitality had been extinguished, it had been "kidnaped" by the maternal energy. Therefore, a partnership where she could maintain a certain emotional distance would fit her comfortably.

Mario was affectionate and agreeable, which Maria Rosa liked very much. However, Maria Rosa's mother never liked him. The mother insisted that her daughter deserved a more educated man; the bad news is that Maria

Rosa agreed with her mother, this was Mario's weak spot. We showed her how difficult it was for her to uphold her choice of a man if he were not vetted by her mother. "It is true -would respond Maria Rosa-, the fact is I would also like him to be more cultured".

We attempted to show her that this is simply living "inside of the maternal discourse", agreeing to a reality seen through mom's disputable lens. We noted to her that when she spoke about Mario, she described him with affection and care.

"Is that true? -Maria Rosa was surprised-, Is that I adore him, but I do not admire him".

Who says he is not admirable? We already knew the answer.

Then, visibly uncomfortable, she told us that for the last several years, Mario had asked her to move to another house, because he felt that the mother-in-law's presence was nefarious for all, and she was intrusive and cruel with their daughter (the four-year-old girl). In addition, he pointed to Maria Rosa she was not assuming her role of housewife and she would not make her own decisions in her mother's presence. We told her perhaps her husband was not as cultured as her mother would like, but he was certainly wise and smart.

For the first time, Maria Rosa listened. She became quiet and snuggled in her armchair. She said she needed a few minutes to organize her thoughts. Of course, we waited. Then she said that just at that moment she understood something she had read in my books. She confessed: "Until a couple of weeks ago -before we started these meetings- when Mario would ask to move someplace else, I would respond to him to move away if he wanted, I would happily remain in this house with my mother and my daughter. Why did I think so? Why did I treat him with such disrespect? ". We told her while observing her image of devoured girl. We could understand. It was evident she had not become the owner of her own desires yet. In addition, it was a miracle that her husband was still by her side, loving her and wishing the best for the family they were building together.

She adjusted herself trying to be more available and attentive. We still need to approach the becoming of her sexuality, her pregnancy, the birth of her daughter Lucia, the post-partum, the baby's first years, the illnesses, the difficulties and the probable delivery of the daughter to the mother. This is what we will establish for the following meetings, however the hypothesis has been drawn.

The prince

Charlie was thirty-six years old Argentine visual artist, in a relationship with Pepa, with whom they have two three-year-old identical twins.

He arrived at the first consultation with his hippy style: wool backpack, an earring in one ear, curly hair neatly braided and green eyes, referred by his partner under threat of divorce. We spoke briefly about our work methodology, and he attempted to tell us that he knew why he was here. However, it was soon clear that he was afraid. We proposed to begin the work of constructing his **human biography**, which would only be successful if he, engaging the most maturity he could muster, wanted to travel along this road. Otherwise, we would cancel the meetings. Obviously, we began by asking about his childhood.

Here is the picture: the maternal family was dominant: great wealth, and historical political power. Charly's father was a physician, from a middle-class family. Historically mom had despised dad and it was always evident that the high lifestyle and economic splurge was supported by mom and her profitable rents. While attempting to tackle his own childhood memories, we arrive at the conclusion that he was a weak child, allergic and sickly. Mom solved the child's suffering buying him toys and anything else he asked for. His brother who was born a year later, will become "the strong", and "with character". Charly appears to be the needy one, instead, his brother Juanpi, was the "bum", the "go-getter", entrepreneur, seductor, and extroverted. There were no memories of an affectionate mom, but a mom who fulfilled every material whim and was the

"Queen of the Universe". She was a beautiful woman, refined, extroverted, educated and enchanting in the social circles. Art and culture were mom's preferred environments. There is where Charly found his vocation.

We asked many times about his experiences as a child, but there were always details about mom; what mom liked and did not like to do; what she spent money on, her decisions, her travels, her problems. Mom was an art collector. We could not make dad appear within this context. He was a normal physician dedicated to his profession, with little glamor when compared with his wife's exuberance. No matter how much we investigated, there were no memories of dad, not even discussions, disagreements or problems between the parents. Plain and simple, dad did not occupy any place at all on this map.

In general terms, we arrived at the conclusion that Charly responded to his mother's wishes. Charly was a timid child who would seclude himself in his lecture and his desire to paint. He felt miniscule next to his mother: an imposing woman, sure of herself. Charly's face was transfixed when speaking of his mother and we pointed out to him that he knew everything about her..., therefore it was very likely that his mother did not know anything about Charly, busy as she was with her power, fame and money.

Effectively, the mother would have liked that Charly were brighter, like Juanpi, with whom she compared him openly. We showed him that to admire such a powerful mother, left him in an impossible position. He had not been loved for the child he had been, but his mother expected to be loved by him.

As it was expected, when inquiring about his school years, he remembered in detail some of the female teachers he feared. Powerful and sure of themselves like his mother.

Did anyone ever help him, or gave him words or facilitated his daily life to help him overcome the fear? No. It never occurred to him to consider this.

By now, we already have a simple image to illustrate his childhood, that of a young child looking at his mother. We showed it to him. It "fit". He felt reflected by the image.

Starting from this "agreement" we approached his adolescence, which as we had anticipated, did not display great charisma.

Effectively, he felt destined to study drawing, painting, sculpture, etching and other artistic techniques. Did he have any relationships with girls? They gave him panic. Did he feel intelligent? Yes, but not handsome. Soon after turning twenty-one, he had his first girlfriend, a fine arts student like himself. For years, his mother had been urging him to confess whether he was homosexual, and if this was the case, she wanted to be the first to know. This left Charly more confused and disabled. It had not crossed his mind; women appeared unreachable. Thus far, we continue to hold the image of a child, weak and smothered by an omnipresent mother.

At this point our role of detectives must get in action by drawing a trustworthy hypothesis. What could we assume? Was he going to select a self-assured partner? Why? Because that was all he knew about the feminine universe. We shared with Charly our "logical conclusion" and we asked him if this first girlfriend was a decisive and strong woman. Charly opened his eyes wide, barely stuttered and confirmed that not only this girlfriend was a powerful woman, but this relationship lasted until he was thirty-two. A ten-tear relationship. We need to investigate - to confirm the character- how did he organize this first and important loving bond.

Looking at mom

Of course, Charly began telling flowery details about this relationship. We stopped listening while observing the image of the weak child controlled by this powerful mother. This image was of more interest that the stories Charly told us. Remember that we are detectives, and we are following our clues.

We asked two or three questions regarding his girlfriend's likely domineering personality and the fear that dominated him. Effectively it was a relationship "dominator-dominated". Charly was in relationship with two strong women: he received money and material comfort from his mother and emotional security from his girlfriend to the extent that Charly submitted to her desires. It is not hard to assume that this scene was the perfect situation for a war between mother and girlfriend. Obviously, the prize booty was Charly. How do we know? Because we follow the logic of the plot. Are we sure this is the case? No, we first generate a hypothesis, then we ask him specifically, so that we can confirm or discard. If it coincides, the client will accept it spontaneously. Only then we will consider it to be true.

We observe together the image of the weak child. We add to this scenario the potential war of desires between mother and girlfriend. The game of desires is played between these two characters; therefore, Charly is not tasked with being in charge. Charly pleased and obeyed both women. It occurred to us the image of a Prince between the Queen Mother and another strong and decisive woman, longing for the throne. He did not like it. We wished each other goodbye and gave him a copy of that image.

At the next encounter he confessed to have been impacted by the image of the prince. He seemed "dumb"

233

without a voice or opinion. However, he remembered scenes that confirmed this role. I showed him the image again and we spent a few minutes looking at it.

Charly told of a few events he remembered -which I will describe here- that confirmed his complacent "character". We decided to continue the story following the chronology. When this first girlfriend left him, he immediately started dating Pepa, the mother of the twins. Is it worth it to ask how is Pepa? No. Right? We, as detectives, already know it. Pepa was going to be a woman planted on her own feet and with well-defined desires. We proposed this, with our hypothesis behind us. We wanted to observe together with Charly, which were the benefits, because it is the benefits that capture us inside the web, not the obstacles. That is why it is important to detect the positive side or what the character obtains while he "feeds" the functioning of the framework. Here we go.

The benefits of being the prince heir of the Great Queen Mother are many. Charly was assured his financial stability; both mom and Pepa provided. One on the material level and the other on the emotional level. He also had all the time in the world to paint, etch, draw, read and study. Of course, Charly had a very charming side: intelligent, cultured, artistic, sensitive, soave and kind. We were missing something regarding the sexual arrangements, if we can call them thus. We could assume that if there were no commitments that required a great degree of responsibility, Charly could charm a woman. Effectively, at the beginning of the relationship, the sex was tender and committed..., until without searching it consciously, Pepa got pregnant. We assume that with the presence of the children, a new "war of desires" would be unleashed because Charly seemed "not to take charge" of his share.

In front of this observation, Charly grumbled some. He defended his masculinity: he had always imagined he would have children, that it was a beautiful time during which they both projected plans into the future and he also decided to continue with the pregnancy. Yes, this was also true. We were trying to find some desire of his own and the maturity to assume the responsibility inherent in any decision.

Continuing with our clues, we share with Charly that from his character as prince, with a strong and willful spouse, the birth of the two girls must have been difficult, and the need of his partner to become softer and surrender to the puerperium. They were going to have to change roles if they both wanted a soft, delicate and protective mother for their children.

The pregnancy was lived with joy, hope and complicity. Charly was a sensitive and intelligent man. It happens in any scenario; the birth of twins tends to be chaotic. Here we have a mother who is accustomed to make decisions and a father more flexible and complacent.

Charly brought some beautiful photos of the twins. We spoke briefly about the girls' current situation, that they were attending a daycare center, about the personality of one and the other and about some disagreements he had with his wife about their rearing. Charly wanted to know our opinion regarding how to set limits for the girls, however this subject was not incumbent upon us. We only intend to observe the reality of his scenario so that he could understand the meaning of each event.

The issue of childrearing overwhelmed Pepa's patience and capacity, who began to express her disagreement regarding Charly's passivity. The more Pepa was upset, the more Charly would shut himself away to play his guitar and

The prince

paint with his oils. Over the first few months, Charly's mother sent a nanny to help at night. Pepa and the nanny ended up fighting since each wanted to do things their own way. Pepa asked Charly to intervene, although he was a peaceful, smiling, delicate man who tried to please his woman, he was unable to resolve a conflict. Then he would disappear from the scene.

We did not obtain this information because Charly told us. No. Truly he did not have any idea of what was happening at home. It was us, as detectives, who, as witness, based on how Charly organized his own tale about a happy family, going to his workshop to paint, we placed words coinciding with the panorama of a woman used to her own autonomy, hijacked by two babies and their cries, nights without sleep, tiredness, demands, availability and exhaustion. We told him what we suspected was happening to Pepa. Charly opened his eyes and would say: "This is the same that Pepa tells me", but as if it were the first time, he figured out the meaning. We invented possible situations with the babies: fevers, snot, nights without sleep, allergies, tiredness, tantrums, seclusion, weariness, fury and some drops of love. The house was total chaos and Pepa was at the end of her rope and her strength. On top of this she felt her husband was farther and farther away, absorbed in an imaginary world of happiness that was not perceived in daily life and more than anything, without noticing that she needed concrete help even if she asked for it at the top of her lungs.

We are naming this, even exaggerating some of the possible scenes so that Charly could be "touched". However, no consideration was excessive enough. At least it helped him get in touch with reality. We looked again at the image of this beautiful, chivalrous prince without responsibilities, to conclude that this splendid sovereign was doing what he knew how to do: take care of himself. He never had the duty to unfold his own desire, he had never worked, he had never been responsible for anything or anyone. The comfort of material abundance enclosed him in a *dolce far niente* that never brought any problems in his life...until he started a family, his wife was overwhelmed by the twins and for the first time she asked him for help. "To help someone else" and "to be in someone else's skin" were completely alien concepts.

We dedicated the following meetings to allocate "reality" on the table. Everyday life. Concrete and palpable needs for each of the babies. Her wife's needs. Money, Schedules. Food. Nights. Rhythms. Routines. Silences. Friendships. Education. Teachers. School. Pediatrician. Fevers. Games. Outings. Nature. This was an alien vocabulary; however, we were bringing Pepa's voice and the children's voices. Charly did not like this at all. Did he have to stop painting or composing music? No. On the other hand, we do not have the authority to tell anyone what they are supposed to do, especially, because we do not know.

But if it was true that in the past, he obtained many and charming benefits from being the son of a powerful mother, now this lavishness was playing against him. What he could do, is observe this scenario and then make any decision he wanted. Then Charly confessed that a couple of months ago, Pepa had thrown him out of the house, although he believed this was a "whim", because his wife was "impulsive" and he was sure "she was going to get over it".

We invited him to look at his image. Sometimes the sovereign places his throne in places far removed from reality. That is why sometimes reality imposes herself without us realizing it beforehand. This is what was happening here: there was suffering and love. Fantasy and reality. Our proposal is to continue looking at the advantages and disadvantages of the scenarios we build.

The brave female boxer

When she consulted our institution, Rosana was the legal clerk at a domestic relations court. She was forty-nine years old and had an eighteen-year-old daughter. She lived with her daughter's father. She had done many years of therapy and decided to try this method out of curiosity. There was nothing specific that worried her, so without much ado, we started with her **human biography**.

She came from a humble family from the outskirts of Buenos Aires. Rosana was the oldest child and seven years later her only brother was born. She had hardly any memories from her childhood. She only knew that when her brother was born, her father left the house and from that moment on there were fierce fighting scenes between the parents. The children were the hostages of these battles. The mother did not want to or could not take care of these children and she "sent" them to the father's house, the father would do the same thing and would "send them" to the mother's house. Of course, the memories are very confused. What she knows is that she changed schools many times, she believes to have attended eleven or twelve different schools during elementary alone, but she was not sure. She remembers to go and come back from school alone and that she stayed in the streets walking around avoiding returning home. This happened both when she had to return to her father's or to her mother's home. She hardly had any memories of her little brother.

The professional named the gravity of the emotional abandonment. Rosana did not have a fixed address nor school nor place of belonging, on top of lacking any kind of oversight. However, there was not an inkling of emotion in her tale. However, she said "she already knew" this from her prior therapies.

We attempted to find out how she remembered herself as a young child. Apparently, she was obsessive with order, timid and very serious. She did not like to be with her mother at her house or with her mother's partner. We asked her why. Then, without the least emotion, she told that starting at the age of ten -somehow, she had absolute certainty about her age at that time- they went to live in a prefabricated home in a poor neighborhood in the periphery of town. They did not have mattresses and slept on some expanded polystyrene mats. The four slept together. The mother placed the children between her and her partner. We explained to her the vicious degree of delivery. She looked at us with a knowing gaze. Of course, at the time began a period of sexual abuse from the stepfather. While he was sleeping, he would touch her. When the mother was absent, he would tell her that he had to give her lessons in sexual education and would teach her how to put on a condom in front of her. She could not remember if her younger brother was there during these events. Despite the impact that these stories produce, we told her that what happened was probably much worse than what she remembers now.

It is important to know that childhood abuses are never remembered exactly how they occurred, because no one names them. This has been described in detail in my books *El poder del discurso materno* and *Amor o dominación. los estragos del patriarcado*. On the other hand, since the childhood experience and that which is named differ so much, the consciousness enters a state of confusion. Therefore, the job of the HBr consists in making order and establishing logic where it is missing.

It is fair to mention that many therapies sometimes name the abuses suffered during childhood. Our interest is to go beyond that. We need to tackle what the individual did with that which happened to us. Because when we are children, we are always victims. But when we become adults, we have the duty to assume responsibility about what we are going to do from here forward. The first step is to have a reality check about what happened to us. The second step is to understand how we survived. The third step is to observe how and when those survival skills begin to prey on our fellow man. The fourth step is to make a positive decision related to love the other despite not having been loved sufficiently. Our proposal is to appeal to the maturity, to the capacity we have as adults to understand ourselves, so that we can understand those who are weaker or more needful than we are.

We continue. The abuse continued for many years. At some point -although she could not tell us at what age-, Rosana tried to place some obstacles to keep her stepfather away, but the following day, he would exact revenge. For example, he would send her to clean the bathroom after soiling the walls with mud and trash. Rosana would cry and would tell her mother that she could not clean all the surfaces, but the mother would tell her that she had to do it and be grateful because the stepfather was educating her, not like her father, who had thrown them out onto the streets. The mother would say the same thing when this man would beat them for any reason, in front of the mother's frozen gaze.

This was the picture: the mother's delivery to a cruel, violent and abusive man, which she called "a good education". To make matters worse, Rosana had to thank him for such a noble service. We spoke with Rosana about her mother's terrible delivery -as well as the father's- the sadism, and cruelty of the adults who should have cared for her. Of course, there were no other adults to whom she could relate what was going on. We explained to her that children search for love and, searching for love, sometimes we find abuse. On those occasions, this minimum of care is the only thing we have, and we do not want to lose it. In that moment, perhaps the first in which she allowed herself a shred of emotion, Rosana agreed saying that this man would always caress her back and she liked that very much. What she detested is what would inevitably follow.

Before greeting her goodbye, we spoke about the destroyed childhood she had lived. We explained that together we would search for her survival mechanism, and we would search for an image to represent it.

There were few options: either she was going to learn to fight -perhaps manipulating or dominating others to win battles- or she would remain bulldozed and forever victimized. We had to search these two clues. For now, we could see a childhood like a floor mop: used, abused, shabby and trampled…We showed her an image that she felt was strong, but she accepted it.

We explained that we would continue the investigation chronologically, to understand how she was able to survive, because all that violence was going to be manifested somehow. She told us that her adolescence had been terrible. We bid each other goodbye.

At the following meeting, we comment that we were left emotionally very "charged", possibly because how distanced she appeared from her own story. We understand that she got used to having to live with those memories, but the objective story was very difficult. Then she told us, somewhat with more emotion, that she was chased by a murky memory she had never related to anyone, that was refreshed with frequency: something disturbing but real. Around thirteen years old, she had cried all night long because of something that left her devastated, she believed she was going to die and since that night she never slept peacefully again. She would be very tired during school and could not concentrate on her studies. We asked her if her stepfather had penetrated her during this period. She cried much and said she did not know. She did not remember. Perhaps but she was not sure. We told her that it did not matter. That her consciousness knew what to split off to tolerate the suffering. Then she calmed down and added that one day she decided to stop resisting and to think that she was not there and to "exit the scene". We told her that this was understandable and that in addition to the horror, most likely she also found in the abuse as small refuge of love. She was surprised. However, she agreed and affirmed: "Yes, it is true, in some way he loved me. He would show jealousy toward other men and that made me feel special".

I want to clarify that the contradiction we feel as individuals who have suffered abuse as children: the certainty that there is a little bit of love there, together with the horror. This unique love is what keeps us inside the abuse when we are already able to leave. This is because the most invisible and terrifying violence is that of **the delivery**. If there had not been delivery by those who were supposed to take care of us, we would not remain within the abuse, because we would not be begging for crumbs of love.

Every time we tackle a human biography where there is abuse of an adult over a child, the detectives have the duty to observe the delivery.

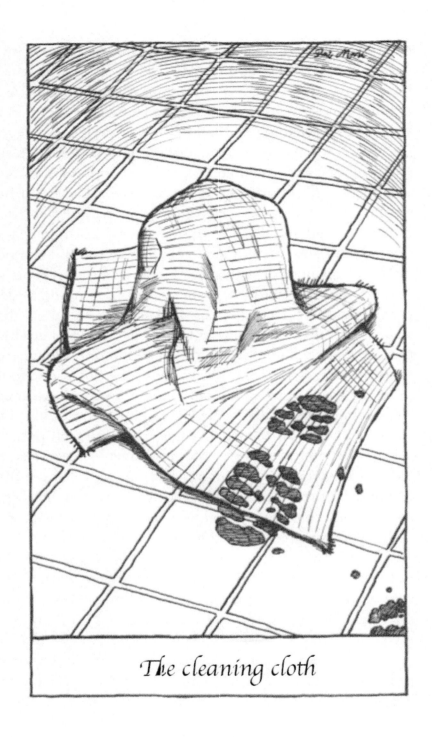

The cleaning cloth

Otherwise, we will never understand the complete dynamic.

After this exchange, Rosana "relaxed" her tension and she set out to tell more details, as if she had permission to let it flow. She remembered that this man was separated by the judiciary from his own children because of accusations of sexual abuse. Her mother knew this. Rosana learned this later because she became friends with the stepfather's daughter, since they were neighbors.

This man used to be visibly violent, but he never hit or yelled at her mother, to the contrary, he was very tender with her. We showed her that this was the principal benefit to the mother and to save herself, she needed to deliver her children. We asked her about her younger brother, and Rosana said that without a doubt, the same happened to him, and she was moved thinking about him.

When she was fifteen, she became pregnant from her stepfather. Her mother took her to the doctor. The story was heartbreaking, not only for the intervention itself, but for the professional's abusive attitude. We will spare you the details, dear reader. They performed the abortion, and she returned home.

Shortly after, Rosana began confronting him. On one occasion since the stepfather would not give her permission to go out with a boy, she threatened him with telling the entire neighborhood about the relationship he had with her. He laughed. Rosana followed suit and the mother punished her. In addition, she assured her: "it was your fault". She could not believe it. She decided to tell her father, who reacted violently: "I will kill him even if I die in prison". Rosana tried to calm him down, she did not want him to kill the stepfather, only to speak with him so that she could go out dancing..., but the father did not do anything at all.

When she was seventeen, she met a boy and left her home. We noted to Rosana, that at this point she had enough confidence in her own ability, her strength and her spirit. Normally, the character "becomes alive" during adolescence. Thus, we will observe in detail which strategies Rosana used when she had more autonomy. With her boyfriend they found a place where to live and they moved together. Pablo worked but she could not understand why he would not bring money to the household. Later she found out that he was hooked on cocaine. They had high voltage relationships and daily fights: blows, beatings and broken dishes. From the beginning she accepted the relationship was like this. They fed each other with beatings and insults.

As detectives, we begin to glimpse which character she is becoming. The active and explicit violence was present in all its forms. Rosana recognized it and wanted to tell of recent anecdotes, but we told her that we will arrive at the present time in an orderly fashion. For now, we could see her character of survival appeared to be of active violence. Someone who could defend herself, even physically and knew how to attack. We showed her the image of a battle-hardened female boxer.

It was logical. She was no longer willing to be a floor mop as she had been during her childhood. Never again. We told her that at our next meeting, we would work with this new image at hand.

During the next meeting we received her with the image printed on paper. She found it funny. She was laughing for the first time, feeling identified and relatively proud.

She told us that, coincidentally, the judgeship where

she was working was dealing with the case of a thirteen-year-old girl who had suffered abuse from her stepfather. She had already read the written arguments and after this meeting the oral arguments were coming. She was moved and lived in a contradiction: how to accuse the abuser and at the same time how to confront the fact that perhaps he was not the only one responsible. We discussed the issue, since there were no cases of precedence nor any book she had consulted where the figure of the one who delivered the child was contemplated. To make matters worse, the defense alleged that the girl lied. Now she could see that there were distortions and misinterpretations galore. In judicial cases, it is also necessary to understand the entire scenario and modify the decisions in favor of the children's true wellbeing.

We continued with the chronology. She lived with Pablo for only three years. He had several women, but she tolerated it while she was developing a strategy on how to move forward, since she did not have another place where to live. She decided to study Law. In the meantime, she found stable employment at a clothing store. When did she separate from Pablo? When she made an agreement with her mother to return to her home -they were in a better economical position than in the past-, until she could finish her career. She was out of the house all day long, between work and study. She almost did not get involved in what was happening with her family and dedicated herself to accomplishing her objective.

As detectives, we listened to her, and we looked out of the corner of our eye at the image of the female boxer. A female boxer…fights. The fights must have been present as a *modus vivendi*. She reluctantly accepted. The question is that she left her mother's home as soon as she graduated:

she was able to pay for a modest rent. During those years she lived with different men. In all those relationships, the fights, the verbal and physical aggressions were frequent. We made a brief tour of the way of relating in each of those relationships and we bid her goodbye until the next meeting.

When she was thirty years old, she met a lawyer a bit older than her. Leonardo. This man was married and had a very good position as an independent attorney. This was a story with an important charge of sexual attraction, in addition to the fights, aggressions, promises and reconciliations. She got pregnant while Leonardo was still married to his wife. He asked her to have an abortion. She threatened him. Finally, what happened was within the logic of the war. We listen to the tales without letting go of observing her image of female boxer, and that each scene fitted the "to kill or to die" pattern.

She got Leonardo to leave his wife and to move in with her. This man belonged to a different socio-economic level: a wealthy family, private schools and universities, the world of polo and golf. Rosana adapted herself rapidly. According to her description, starting at that moment she lowered her aggression and decided to attempt a more peaceful relationship, taking everything that Leonardo was willing to give her: basically, an economic backing and a relaxed and safe universe. During this impasse, she told him of the abuse she had suffered during her childhood at the hand of her stepfather and, consequently, Leonardo asked her not to visit her mother again. In exchange he promised her protection and shelter.

Pamela's pregnancy was difficult. Under this scenario, nothing different could have happened. She had to have rest to avoid a miscarriage.

The brave female boxer

Regardless, Leonardo took care of her and asked that she take a year leave. Observing this panorama, the idyllic situation with Leonardo did not fit with the image, therefore we had to review where this contained force and aggression were going to be displayed.

Obviously, she had a C-section. Let's look at the girl's early childhood. This was complicated because, when a client is the mother of a "dark" adolescent with piercings all over her face, she does not feel like remembering the baby stages. It seemed so far away and out of context…However, it is there where we will find valuable information. We must remember that during the vital crises -and the period of raising children always is- our characters bring up their best attributes.

In fact, Pamela was a child who figured out how to take care of herself. How did we know? Because the mother assured us: "She was such a good child that she did not cause me any work", we already know she is an over-adapted child who takes care of her mother overwhelmed by conflicts and preoccupations. We explained to her that this is another form of abuse. It was not sexual abuse, of course. But she was not taking care of resolving her daughters' needs while she was busy trying to resolve her own, forcing the girl to be on the lookout for her. She understood perfectly.

Once the real panorama had been brought up, Rosana could relate many episodes where she would explode in front of anyone's smallest misstep: the bus driver, the bank teller, or the cleaning lady. Pamela was witness of her mother's explosions, which Rosana was not aware, not even to tamper the fury. Together we look at the image of the female boxer. We agreed that to win, the female boxer had to strike first, just in case. Rosana was impacted, as if for the first time she registered the power of her automatic behavior.

We had already confirmed her character. We already knew that her capacity to box had been her essential mechanism of survival and, that from her childhood experience she has always felt in danger, and therefore, to defend and attack were her emotional safety pass. Now we needed to review and observe with new eyes the different episodes, important or subtle, so that Rosana would have full consciousness of how she could daily hurt those she loved most. This was our working hypothesis: to evaluate if it was true that in the present moment she was in danger, or if she behaved from her infantile automatic reaction. Then she would be free to make any decision she wanted.

This is how the following meetings were spent, when she would tell with astonishment, her own disproportionate aggressive attitudes. In the beginning she realized she knew hardly anything about Pamela's life, her only child. She attempted to approach her lovingly, but Pamela rejected her. This was logic, she was in the middle of her adolescence. Then she sent her some messages through Facebook telling her about some of the painful episodes of the period when her daughter was in elementary school and asking her for forgiveness for having left her so alone. She wrote to her that she remembered her crying begging her not to send her to a camp the school had organized, even as Rosana at that time ignored her pleading, she sent her anyway and never found out what had happened, because the child refused to tell her. Pamela had found refuge in her guitar; she had finished high school but did not have any thoughts about a future career and had few friends. After a few weeks, she managed a small rapprochement and she proposed to invite her best friend to a short vacation they had planned with the family. Pamela agreed and was a little bit more communicative with her mother.

During the last meetings we tackled her relationship with her partner, we will not discuss here. The integration of both worlds has been complex, and the age difference was more evident as time went on. We saw that she continued to spend her energy fighting with her mother, which was stolen from her relationship with her partner and her daughter. Rosana began to commit to this emotional path with surprising courage. She unabashedly spoke of her most unpleasant aspects. She was only interested in healing and fixing, to be more loving with her daughter and her fellow human beings.

One day, she came to the consultation and related with pride that her daughter Pamela had asked her to sleep with her in her bed. The most surprising part is that Rosana accepted willingly! -something unthinkable a few months ago- under her husband's astonished gaze, who did not know what to think of the changes his wife was implementing. We celebrated that Pamela felt deserving and could finally! Ask for something she needed since she was little. And, of course, that Rosana would simply accept it without discussion as it had happened before. She could feel Pamela's fragility, her fears, her uncertainties, and the loneliness that kept her isolated from her peers.

Shortly after, she came to bid a final goodbye to her HBr. She was happy with the work she had accomplished, but mostly the clarity of what remained to be done. She was aware that, despite having lived a heart-rendering childhood, it did not serve her to remain in an attitude of permanent vengeance. On the other hand, she recognized the abandonment and the lack of listening she had inflicted on her daughter were not that different from what she had suffered as a child. She to devote every day wanted to reverse this. Even as the court clerk she modified the reading of court records, listening to the parties with more maturity and understanding, attempting to collaborate so that each adult would assume their share of responsibility. The **human biography** was on its way.

The slave

Josefina was thirty-three and had a newborn baby. She was a mathematics professor at several schools and was currently on maternity leave. She was worried about several things, particularly her psoriasis, that was first detected when she was nine years old and would wax and wane in severity at different times. It had worsened since the baby was born. She also wanted to better understand her relationship with her mother, since the birth of her son she had felt many internal contradictions.

After a pleasant exchange, we began the inquiry on her **human biography**. Her mother was originally from Misiones, on the Argentine northeastern region. When she finished high school, she moved to Buenos Aires to find work. Her father was the superintendent of a building and the youngest of six children. He orphaned as a child and was not able to finish high school because he worked since he was very young, although he advanced until he owned his own business.

Her parents met through work and have three children. Josefina is the oldest, named as the responsible and accommodating one. Then came a brother who was named as the mother's favorite, and the younger brother was named the rebel without a cause.

Josefina wanted to tell us about a great childhood, but we started asking specific questions about the home environment, the mother's personality and her own memories, until it became clear that mom lived complaining about dad. She stopped working when she married and discharged her pain and rage against her children. The mother would say that the father "held her prisoner" because he was possessive and jealous.

We asked if the parents are still living together. Yes. Then this dynamic between mom and dad is the result of an agreement between them. Josefina was shocked with this point of view about the issue, since she had always believed in "poor mom, her lot is a difficult life". We understood this to be the maternal discourse, this is what mom had repeated throughout her childhood, and this is how Josefina adopted as true.

Josefina's childhood had been flooded with mom's complaints. Even if mom was "very good": she helped at the local parish and all the neighbors loved her. This was likely to have happened. This is why we asked specifically what happened inside the home. Little by little memories surfaced about all of Josefina's duties she was required to do at home: clean and organize the home, and care for her brothers. Even after she had cleaned, her mother would hit her if she considered the result to be less than expected. There were no memories about the father, apparently, he worked a lot, and in addition, when the fights began between the parents, he would slam the door and leave. Where? Josephine had no idea, but she never questioned.

We asked her where she thought she found some affection and understanding. She thought, reflected, searched…, but there were no memories.

Instead, she remembered many instances in which, since she was responsible for cleaning, had attempted that her brothers did not make a mess. The problem appeared when they fought among themselves and would throw around all the toys and she tried to make them stop. Of course, when mom returned, it was Josefina who received the beatings.

She did not have problems at school, she had two girlfriends with whom she still maintains a relationship. On the other hand, at home there was no social life or extended family. The childhood panorama was clear: there was a mother looking at herself and leaving the oldest daughter in her place, to be responsible for the household and the care of her brothers. The father was absent from the scenario. We show her a recurrent image, of a girl looking at her mother and attempting to calm her.

Josefina looked at it and said that to this day it continued being so. She still felt the duty to care for her mother and her siblings.

We briefly explained to her how the abuse dynamics works (everything is written in my book *Adicciones y violencias invisibles*) and we assured her that we would investigate until we found how far has the havoc of this abuse reached, because when a young girl protects her mother, and later she becomes an adult, she continues protecting…, there is no room to take care of another. She just had a baby. Therefore, we are starting to see the problem. We greeted her goodbye.

Josefina returned two weeks later. She asked if we believed that it was wrong that she stayed at her mother's house since the baby was born. We explained to her that we do not pass judgment on anything or anybody. On the other hand, we had only discussed her childhood, but if we continued the investigation, we would most likely be able to globally understand her life history, and she would have more tools to make her own decisions.

She related that after the first meeting, her psoriasis worsened. There were periods in which the condition was more active and others in which it was more latent.

Looking at mom

She thought it could be related to having "touched" painful aspects of her childhood. We told her that we did not know yet, but in principle, when the skin suffers so much, it has to do with the absolute lack of maternal body contact and with an intense need for caresses and pampering. Yes, you may say that all human beings should have skin conditions because we all have had a lack of physical contact. It is true, we are the fruit of miraculous survival.

We decided to continue with the chronology. She always knew that mathematics was easy for her. She studied and liked to go out to dance. She said her mother always gave her permission. This seemed strange. We asked her if the mother began to take care of the house or if she had outside help. Josefina was surprised. She never thought something like that. It was obvious this was not the case. She continued to oversee the house cleaning, since this was the condition to be able to go out. Even on Saturdays, the day of general cleaning. First, she had to fulfill her obligations and then she could go out. We told her this was not "not having problems with having permission to go out to dance". To the contrary. This seemed slave work. The mother did not bother to take care of her, nor did she find out where she was going at night nor with whom. She only wanted someone who could clean the house, which obviously the mother did not want to assume. Then we show her the image of slavery.

In truth, she felt locked up, even if she had the "freedom" to come and go as she wished. The mother never asked her where she went or at what time she returned home if the house was in order. She never talked to her or suggested that she take care of herself. The emotional abandonment was confirmed. On the other

261

hand, Josefina understood that if she did not take care of herself, nobody was going to take care of her. At fourteen she had her first boyfriend, with whom she began her sexual life. It was strange, she knew little or nothing, and it seemed "dirty" what she was doing, but she did not tell anyone.

What happened with the psoriasis? Did her mother take her to a doctor? Was anyone interested? Did it itch? Was she ashamed? Did she hide it? Josefina was unable to respond. She did not remember seeing a doctor, but she knew that what she had on her arms and legs was psoriasis and that she should not touch it. She believed it was the cleaning products that caused the skin lesions and dreamt that when she would be older, she would stop cleaning and the problem would disappear. We asked her if it was an impediment in the relationships with her boyfriends, and she did not know how to respond. She also did not know why she related the psoriasis to the cleaning products. We assumed that the mother may have mentioned the issue and she took it as true.

Then, moved, she added: "Now I understand that I did not have a mother, I always took care of myself. Then she asked me: why am I still so attached to her? Why do I need her so much? I go to her house every day, and I do everything I can to make her happy, I bring her gifts, but she continues not having any interest in me".

We responded to her that the wounded girl believes that the more she cleans and the more she satisfies her mother, sometimes she was going to deserve to be loved. However,…this is an infantile illusion. All children deserve to be loved. Unfortunately, the adults are not capable of loving (the children or anyone else). This is the truth. The adults are not capable of loving; however, nobody, and

262

much less a child, must do anything to be deserving of love.

We also told her that we were surprised that she never dared "rebel" against those duties imposed by her mother since she was a child; moreover, as she was growing up and learning about different situations, she never took the decision to stop responding to those mandates. However, apparently, her skin would constantly say "no". It really fits well the image of the slave who has resigned herself to her fate believing her destiny is unchangeable. If we observe our hypothesis -assuming that we are correct and we have a slave bleeding through her skin- it is possible that the few moments of "freedom" she experienced them in secret. She would hide, minimize or forget them. If we draw a few clues to define where are we going to continue our investigation; "freedom" in any form would produce feelings of guilt or she was going to feel she did not have the right, or she was going to have to pay a high price to obtain it. Being detectives, we are interested in imagining the logic of a scenario, before continuing to listen to the client. We needed to understand the subjectivity of a slave to be able to comprehensively get into the character.

We told her so. She understood and was moved. She even calculated for the times when her psoriasis strongly flared up to see if they coincided with times when she took better care of herself, she was aware that she could not clean so much, she would seclude herself or would allow herself permission to work less.

When she finished high school, she enrolled at the university to study mathematics. Now she realizes that this was a period when she felt excessively "free". We asked her if during that period she had stopped cleaning the house. No, "this" continued as usual. However, in some way being around her new companions made her "feel" better.

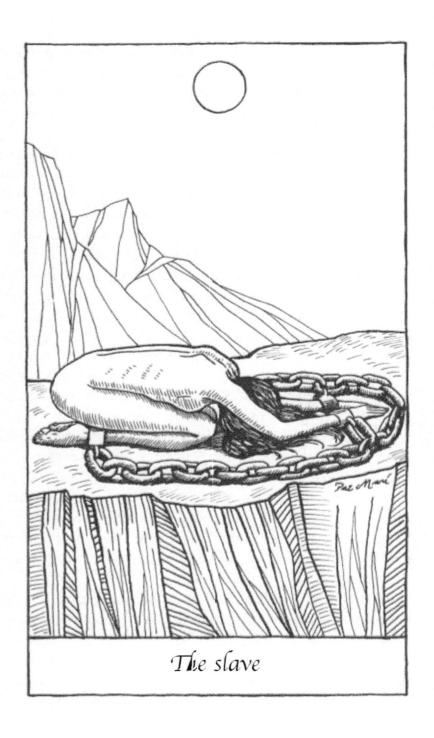

The slave

During this period, she had a few boyfriends, although there is little to relate about those relationships. We asked her about the psoriasis, but apparently it was part of her being, she carried her hurt skin with her.

Of course, the mother could not forgive Josefina for dedicating "to herself" and that she would "forget" about her family while she was studying. This generated much guilt to the slave, and therefore, over the weekends, she would double on her efforts regarding the cleaning, the cooking, the clothing and anything she could leave shining in her family home.

When she was twenty-eight, Josefina already had a good situation: she held several jobs as teacher and tutored a group of private students. During this period, she got reacquainted with a university friend and they started dating. This was Ernesto, her current husband.

If we are detectives...what clues are we going to observe if she is a slave? What kind of man is she going to establish a relationship with? Two options arise: either she will find a submitter with whom she can "shine" in her slave costume, or she would make alliance with an obedient, appeased and un-demanding man, so that she can continue to respond forever more to mom's insatiable needs.

We only needed to ask her which one of the two options "fit" Ernesto.

Josefina could not believe it. She had never considered it in this light, but "it was ripe for the taking". It was obvious to her that Ernesto was an obedient and docile man who responded submissive to the demands from his own mother. For example, he adored nature, he would have wanted to study Agronomy or Ecology, but he had to study Economy under strict requirement by his parents. He was also complacent and kind with Josefina, and without a doubt those qualities endeared him to her. Until now we have a young couple, living in harmony within the same system of abuses, without spreading too far any personal desire, or, in any case, paying a high price.

Both worked a lot and decided to move together. How do you think the sexuality of this couple would be? Possibly with quiet agreements, without great passion but also without conflicts. I insist that the detectives first organize the hypothesis and then we check with the client to confirm if we are on the right track. This exercise is important, because if we ask openly about "how is the sexual life with your partner", we will all describe feats that are difficult to confirm. It is not that we care much, but people's sexual lives are a form of expression, in line with other aspects of their lives. The same things happen in bed as in other areas. These are clues and as such they must coincide. In this case, there were agreements. Possibly they both preferred to sacrifice themselves a little bit not to have to endure problems, complaints or threats. They were both wounded and had learned to obey, to be quiet, to resolve and then sleep peacefully.

Josefina was an extremely intelligent young woman; at each meeting she would relay many thoughts she linked to her slavery, her fears, the punishments she received and the accommodation to a reality she had never dared to challenge.

The pregnancy elapsed without problems. Does a slave complain? She did not have pains or inconvenience except for the usual during the last month. She worked until the week before giving birth to have more time off after the baby was born. She had a short and intense delivery. She never lost control. We traveled along the details of her return home until Josefina interrupted: "I know what is happening to me. Do you know who my skin reacts against? Against my mother! My mother had established that I had to be at her house during the first month. She dictated it and I accepted it. Ernesto thought it was fine. From the hospital, Ernesto brought me to my parents' home. Why? My mother doesn't even help me. I miss my husband. My skin is worse than ever. At night I am afraid that my mother would be bothered when then baby cries. Why did I go to her house? Why? Why?

Josefina was crying and laughing at the same time. This was a good beginning. Why? Perhaps because a slave does not ask questions? What would happen if you began to ask? What price do you have to pay? Josefina answered with certitude. "No price at all. This issue of paying with my work is a subject of the past. I don't have to pay for anything. I do not have debts. Today I go back with my child to my own home. What ridiculous things we do!".

This was the beginning of a beautiful awakening.

The donkey with blinders

Maria de los Angeles was an Argentine woman living in Mexico City. These meetings were held via videoconference. She was fifty-three years old when she began her first consultation. She was married with two sons aged twenty-three and twenty. She had a degree in social work but worked as administrator in a large firm. She also participated in a study group with psychology professionals in her area and learned about my books from one of her colleagues in the group. She wanted to grant herself the opportunity to experience the construction of her **human biography**. In addition, she wanted to find out why she felt such rejection towards her mother. Living away from her country of birth, she had noble feelings toward her. The problem arose each time they met in person.

We started with her childhood. The mother came from a humble family. The father, on the other hand, was from a family of intellectuals, although he worked at different firms since he was young. The father suffered chronic depression until his death. The mother did not work and was always at home; she was a cold and distant woman. Maria de los Angeles had difficulties with her studies, but she did not have anyone to offer her support; in addition, her mother was always busy. She and her brother would ask to be taken to the park across the street, but the mother never consented; sometimes when the father would return from work and was not suffering from a headache, he would take them to the park.

We asked her who provided her with affection. She thought for a little while and said, "from no one". She

269

immediately began describing her mother's violence. When Maria de los Angeles would fight with her brother, the mother would first threaten them, then she would search for a belt to hit them both. When the beating was over, the mother would ingest a Valium and go to bed.

We pointed out that when we asked her about affection, she related this scene. Therefore, we could assume that through this modality she found a way to receive "affection" and be "touched" by the mother. She was shocked. She thought that said in this manner, "this" was too shocking. Later she recognized those were the only occasions when her mother looked at her. We also asked her about the father, it seems he beat them also, but less because he was at home less often.

We spoke about the havoc created by violence against children, about the aridity to enter life under these conditions, and we were clear that we had to review the mechanisms she had later utilized to counter the violence she had received.

She attended high school at a parish school; it appears she had several girlfriends with whom she could go out. She remembered the exact day when her mother pounced on her to beat her. Maria de los Angeles was seventeen, she stopped her hand and told her: "If you hit me one more time and you will never see me again". Effectively, it was the last time she received a beating. We told her we did not have a way to confirm if this had been so -the detectives know that the memories are organized based on deceived discourses- in any way it was an interesting piece of information: she seemed to be a "decisive" youth.

Around this time, she met Alberto, her current husband. They began their relationship but did not have sexual relations until they got married, eight years later. We offered some words about the subject, that it must have been a complicated issue. Possibly, having learned to distance herself from her emotions and from her body not to suffer the maternal violence, this distance was going to be manifested in her sexual life. Maria de los Angeles was interested in this "view" but could not quite understand it.

She studied Social Sciences at the university without difficulty. Alberto was a businessman and worked with his own father. Maria de los Angeles' mother would not welcome her boyfriend "who did not attend college". They got married when they had saved enough money and which coincided with Alberto accepting a job offer in Mexico, and this is how they left.

At this point, we told her that eight years of engagement was a long time, however, in this tale there was no mention of anything related to love, passion, vitality, fights, hopes or dreams. She then clarified that those years of engagement were filled with fights, "something normal for a couple". Why did they fight? Because Alberto did not agree with what she was studying. We were surprised that she minimized something that is so fundamental in a person's life: nothing more than what we want to undertake in life. If our own vocation comes into confrontation with the person who loves us and with whom we have a life project together, something complicated is taking place. She thought about it and responded that it was true, she had brushed it off then as now.

As detectives, it is important to observe that this is how Maria de los Angeles had learned about affective relationships: through fights and aggression. Then she told several anecdotes that confirmed their mutual contempt, the lack of interest between them and their emotional distance. We greeted her goodbye letting her know that

271

during the following meeting we would verify if freezing was her principal mechanism to protect herself from suffering.

We made note in our detective notebook that we were working with a woman married for the last thirty years and the alliances and primary agreements between her and her husband were based on working, sacrifice, work and work. They must possibly understand each other on this level, and if we confirmed it and if this environment is working, the conflicts would not arise within the couple. In this case, it is likely that the children must have endured most of the suffering, at least during childhood.

What it the purpose "to write down" these thoughts? Because we need to imagine a scenario utilizing the few elements we have, to be able to establish the possible "clues". Otherwise, during the next meeting we are going to ask her "how are you doing?" and be subjected to deceived responses that are not going to help, instead of going directly to the two or three hypothesis we have, which must be confirmed. I insist that the detective's work continues outside of the actual meetings with the clients. Like strategists who think and work beyond the times of action. This allows us to clear our minds, organize the pieces we have and define how we will continue the investigation.

During the next meeting, Maria de los Angeles wanted to tell us that she had been thinking, that what she liked best was to be left alone. People bothered her. She did not like to live in Mexico; therefore, she liked living in "her own world". She seemed to be a hard and distant woman. But we responded that it was understandable, thinking that it was a reasonable mechanism to survive a difficult childhood. We decided to continue with the chronology.

The couple moved to Mexico City; this was very difficult for her; she could not find, nor did she try to integrate into the community. Sometimes she had the fantasy of returning to Buenos Aires, but at the same time, she realized she did not have anything interesting there either. In the beginning Maria de los Angeles and her husband, took on all sorts of difficult jobs. They were very focused in their economic progress. They shared this hope.

Of course, the fights between them continued endlessly. The worse battles happened when Maria de los Angeles wanted to attend a master's degree program at the university, as she never gave up on the opportunity to develop her profession. Around this subject we are not yet clear about the image we will show her. There was tenacity, hardness and sacrifice. There was also sufficient strength to sustain the fights. But we were not sure, which is something we shared with her. We decided to continue and see if we could gather more elements to complete the picture.

A few years after emigrating, her first child was born. Why? Was there desire? Complicity? They simply thought that it "was appropriate". Three years later their second child was born. Both children by scheduled C-Section. She did not breast-feed (in these cases the excuses are multiple, we do not care, nor it is worth listening to them, because it is obvious that, if we are looking at a hard and tenacious image…, it does not fit with the softness of milk-filled breasts). Of course, in both cases she returned to work very quickly. Work is sacred.

When we are constructing **human biographies** and the children are born, we always attempt to approach the experience from the children's point of view. Because this will complete the panorama, although in this case it was easy to realize that these children were not going to receive

273

anything soft, tender, protective or welcoming from the mother. It was impossible. It only remained to ask what the recurring manifestations of those children were. Of course, they were often sick. When the second child started school, he had a fever every day! And she had to go pick him up at the kindergarten. The children are so wise! When he arrived home, the fever miraculously disappeared.

During those moments we wanted to offer her an image strong enough so that Maria de los Angeles could observe her naked reality.

We showed her a donkey with blinders: working, going forward and blind to anything happening around her.

We had the feeling that she "advanced" without looking around, without looking at her children, without looking at herself. "Worked", "went", "did", cut off from her emotional world, and therefore from her children and husband's emotional universe. The solitude she hoped for kept her safe from having to connect with anyone. The problem we could glimpse is that we would not be able to find much more in this scenario, because "since she did not want to see" and only going to work as the only objective, her "range" appeared narrow.

She agreed. She felt like that: working and "pulling ahead". Isolated from everybody. She related certain episodes and a request from her husband that confirmed this hypothesis. Later we had other meetings in which we took apart each of her children's childhood. When the children are adults, we feel unmotivated. However, it is very important work. During each night of heartbreak lived by our children when they were little, are the seeds of future events in the current family situations. This is what we did with Maria de los Angeles; we started finding very painful episodes from the children's point of view. Let's imagine

The donkey with blinders

the two creatures with a mother who works and works and does not see anything beyond her nose! It must have been very frustrating. Then we arrive at the present time, when Maria de los Angeles recognizes that she holds a distant and superficial bond with her sons. They were both attending university, they lived on their own and she knew absolutely nothing about them.

She also recognized that in all the prior therapies she had attended, since her "problem" were the eternal fights she had with her husband, that was the focus. However, she had never approached the relationship with her sons, because in her mind, "it was not a problem". It was sad to confirm that, looking at the entire scenario, it was obvious that these sons -now young adults- must have been reclaiming everything for a long time. How can we not take them into consideration! Perhaps this could be a way to remove her blinders, at least for a little while.

A few meetings later, Maria de los Angeles requested a meeting outside the regular schedule. She was scared. The oldest son had a strong discussion with his father, who yelled at him that he was ungrateful for everything he had received. The young man responded desperate that he wanted to kill himself and was going to do so. The father was upset and continued to accuse him, told Maria de los Angeles: "let's go, we are going to be late" (they had arranged an outing with friends). Maria de los Angeles did not know what to do. She was doubting! Do you realize this, my dear readers, how the lack of love works? This is not a judgement about courage. It is to look at the logic of the donkey with blinders and understand that she cannot "see beyond". She was unable to feel her son's historical desperation. She does not dare going outside her usual rut. She does not know another path than the one she takes every day of her life. She is disoriented because something different has happened. The destiny is removing the blinders with fury and the light is blinding. I want to demonstrate that we are observing "this" scene inside of "this scenario.

In the middle of this piercing incident, the young man looked at his mother and said: "Please stay with me". Maria de los Angeles finally made the decision. She understood that she needed to remain there. The father was furious. The son hugged her crying and said: "This is the first time in my life you chose me. Thank you". The HBr was crying when listening to the story, but Maria de los Angeles remained stoic in front of the computer screen.

We had encouraged her to go a little bit further. She needed to remove her blinders, look around (not very far, just look at her children), but also walk on different, new paths. This is what she began to do with much difficulty. She began timidly talking with this son, sharing something about this investigation she was starting with a professional that lived in Argentina. She showed him the image of the donkey with blinders, she explained to him how she was observing the family history with new eyes and how she did not have the tools to love them with care in the past. She told him that now she is coming to see reality and that still everything feels too complex. She told him without many details some anecdotes from her own childhood. She initiated a minimal dialog. With each meeting, each silent gaze toward her children, were experienced as she had scaled mount Everest. This is why she needed support and the strength of her HBr, but the path had been set.

The cave

Maximo was sixty-four years old, he was a title officer, was married, had a twenty-seven-year-old daughter and a three-month-old grandson. At first sight, he was elegant, with black eyes and thick beard but very uptight. He was unwilling to answer general questions because he had come with a very precise problem he needed to tackle and according to him, it was of a sexual matter. He had done psychoanalysis for twenty-five years -since his daughter's birth- and according to his words, he would have been unable to support his family or progress professionally without that help. A colleague had recommended my book *Amor o dominación. Los estragos del patriarcado* and he decided to try this new method.

He considered himself a pornography addict. He wished to talk about multiple justifications and "solutions" that had been recommended to him throughout his life, but we were not interested. We explained that our work was going to be concentrated in finding his "shadow", detecting his character and understanding his survival mechanisms, and that we would attempt to look at his scenario in the broadest possible manner without falling prey of easy interpretations. We could not guarantee any "solution". We could begin the path together and see how far we could go. He agreed.

These interviews were done via videoconference, since Maximo resides in the city of Salta, in the Argentine northwest. His mother came from a fervent catholic family. His father had been a title officer, just like his grandfather, also of catholic families. They hay seven sons. Maximo was

279

the oldest. Initially we inquired about the father's figure, because he may have exerted a significant influence on Maximo, and without a doubt he responded: "He was an authoritarian, as soon as he would arrive at the house, you could not hear a pin drop, the air would get heavy, he yelled about everything, he was very sexist, he despised women, among them my mother. I feared him very much, sometimes I hated him…". We asked if the father beat him. He said no. We told him we did not believe him. In a panorama like this, there must be beatings. Then he answered: "Well, yes, sometimes, but not too many. Only if we made him mad".

I want to demonstrate once more how the "forgetfulness mechanism" comes into action (this is described in detail in my book *Adicciones y violencias invisibles*). Therefore, the detectives need to "name" with clear and unequivocal words what the logic shows but the individual cannot remember. Or does not know. He may have lived many happy or miserable experiences, but if they were not named, the consciousness cannot organize them. If there is no organization, there are no memories. This is why I continue to insist on the extreme importance I place on the "construction" the detective can build looking at the map's logic.

Why does it matter if the father beat him or not, if he was an abuser? Because when we add together the pieces that are missing -the beatings and the blows, for example- the individual can glimpse with more coherence and conviction the dimension of his emotional abandonment, or the violence exerted over the child he has been. On the other hand, once we name that there were punishments and consequently the individual only remembers one episode, slowly other episodes will appear, and then others, until a waterfall of gushing memories will provide a realistic scenario.

Let us return to our protagonist. He remembered himself as very timid, and he did not like to go to school. Right away he began talking again about how fearsome his father had been. Then we asked him directly, what was his mother doing during these circumstances, since she was the other adult in the house. Did she do anything to impede this from happening? Maximo was taken aback and stuttered: "She would not do anything".

What I am writing may seem trivial...I insist this is the inescapable task of the detective. I have explained that the mothers are the owners of the official discourse, therefore...the mothers rarely appear as the executioner. Basically, because we do not name ourselves as such. It is true that the father was cruel, but he was in clear collusion with the mother. The mother was as scary as her husband, although not as visible. We explain to Maximo that the drama of emotional abandonment in which his mother had left him, served on a platter, so that the father could discharge his cruelty on him. We are not judging anybody. Most likely the mother had lived horrendous situations during her early childhood, the father as well, and so many generations back. This is why, it is imperative to begin naming the maternal emotional abandonment.

We spoke for a long time about these concepts, which Maximo listened to between intrigued and uncomfortable. Until he finally accepted, adding that the mother had been a very cold woman, who had never been emotionally close to any of her children. Perhaps by maintaining an army of seven fearful children she guaranteed that none of them would ever dare ask her for anything. He continued remembering that, when there was an affectionate teacher who approached him to give him a kiss, he considered this was something bad. Of course, affection and physical contact bordered on sin.

Beyond the mother's coldness and the father's punishments, we shared with Maximo some hypotheses; we assume that since he was little, he was keenly aware of his own desires. We are not talking about sexuality, but his own "internal fire". An innate force. We suppose that the mother had been very cruel with him, faced with the possibility that something in this original, different, crazy desire…would appear. It is possible that he did not remember anything about this, in addition we are talking about something very subtle, there was nothing concrete. But we were going to name the desires, expectations, or intimate hopes. We also thought important to search if at any time a different vocation had surged. When a child is born with a clear internal freedom or with the feeling that he "does not belong to his own family", and this family is extremely authoritarian, normally the child falls into a torrent of threats and mandates, until he is silenced.

If this happens before puberty, it is possible that the child will not retain any memory or sensation that links him to "that part" of himself. Then we could imagine this child burning inside. This is not a genital fire. It is pure desire, it is the sense of life, it is the perception of something big inside himself. He could have had experiences like a caged animal. Until he exhausted his strength and fell asleep forever. The problem with trying to confirm all this, is that he does not know it. He does not remember. We explain this because, in the beginning we are going to remove the fire from his genitality, which is where he was looking for too many years. We need to stop glancing though the keyhole if we expect to understand something relevant about his life.

Maximo was very moved, and he held back his tears. He needed a few moments to regain his composure. Then he talked about a few episodes that confirmed that the mother functioned as the father's "associate". He remembered that the mother made fun of him with sarcasm. Then he remembered atrocious punishments I will not describe here.

This is how he spent his childhood and adolescence. Like his brothers, he studied at a religious school. We proposed that starting with his youth we were going to investigate how did he survive the emotional abandonment. We formulated different questions about how his relationships with friends and what he liked, until he named his extreme timidity. During adolescence, this became a heavier burden. He was so withdrawn that some people considered him rude, since he could not even greet people. During that time, he began to masturbate a lot. We told him that nobody could define what is "a lot". Perhaps this is all a withdrawn adolescent could do. We asked for his vocation, but he did not have "any idea". Obviously, he studied law because it had been already decided that he would work in his father's offices. By now, Maximo was exhausted and tense, so we greeted him until next time.

During the following virtual meeting, we had already prepared an image to show him and see if it fit. We presented him with the drawing of a man inside a cave. He said he felt identified with the image. It was exactly like that, he was trapped. Later you will see the meaning of also having drawn his internal fire.

We decided to continue with the chronology. He completed his studies in solitude. He would not speak with anyone, did not have friends, did not practice sports, did not go out on the weekends. We tried to find out about his sexual life, although we believe to have the answers. He finishes his studies. At age twenty-four, he had his first connection with a woman, but did not have sexual relations with her. In any event, it was the first time he received a caress from anyone. He still remembered her with much fondness.

Later he had other girlfriends, but his sexual life was difficult, he had the fantasy that he could hurt them. He had much desire for them in his imagination, but when he was in front of them, he was paralyzed. Later he preferred to masturbate by himself. We return to our first hypothesis explaining that he appeared to be a man with many desires, more than what could fit in the interior of a cave. As if there was a ball of fire inside waiting to come out and express itself, but it was trapped and fearful of his own possible explosion. It fit him. He said that those words came closer to what he was feeling inside but did not know how to explain. It is important for us to look at a sketch about his functioning. We felt that this internal fire was locked up, contained, and that of necessity, it was going to search for alternative paths to manifest itself.

When he was thirty-four, he met Felisa, his wife. We inquired about what made him fall in love with Felisa. He could not answer, except that she was the right kind of woman. There was no desire, passion or good sex. Felisa was an economist; she had a good job and was self-sufficient. The best part is that she did not demand anything from him. This was an interesting piece of information, because it provides evidence that the biggest benefit was that this woman did not ask him to abandon the cave.

The cave

His infantile fear was the protagonist of this scenario. Just now he began to trust the HBr. He said this was the first time he did not feel judged or pressured. We continued asking about the intimacy in the marriage. There was nothing at all, except for a life without commotion. Felisa was very attached to her own parents, and therefore she would leave Maximo "in peace", who did not even have to tolerate her demand to take care of her emotionally. A few years later, the only daughter of the marriage was born, also named Felisa, but she was called "Feli" to distinguish her from her mother. At this moment, Maximo wished to discharge multiple complaints about his wife, especially related to the historical alliance his wife had forged with their daughter, against him. We preferred to wait, since we were observing the "nothing" in this couple's relationship.

Looking at the image, there is a man enclosed in his own cave not to enter in contact with his own power. This was going to generate isolation and was going to invite him to remain ignorant about anything else that happened around him. Any time a client brings up complaints, it is our duty as detectives to look at the entire scenario, since each character contributes to the movements of the play in which all others participate. If there is a secluded man, what is everyone else going to do? They will gather among themselves and will keep each other company as best they can outside of the seclusion. If we continue contemplating the image and we compare it with his motive for the consultation; isn't it logical? Masturbating is what a person has available to feel well if he is completely alone. Till now…the pieces of the puzzle fit.

Maximo could hardly tell us anything about Feli's childhood. It was not surprising that he answered in a conventional manner, from "she was a beautiful girl" to "she did well in school", or "she had a special touch for music". We are not saying that these things are not true, but we are looking for a deeper understanding of his daughter that he obviously never acquired. His daughter was already married and had recently become the mother of a boy. Maximo had to acknowledge that the relationship he had with his daughter and son-in-law was superficial. The world unfolded very far away from his cave, that still held him prisoner of his childhood fears.

Maximo was a trust officer with a solid financial position and a well-established professional recognition; however, his affective and intimate capabilities were stuck in his earliest childhood. We showed him how he had spent his adult life without any committed emotional relationships and the two people closest to him, his wife and his daughter, had not been able to pierce through the cave's walls, that kept him, until now, protected from the fearful child he had been. Therefore, we were not going to listen to his complaints.

He got uncomfortable, thought about it and remembered an episode of a fight between his wife and his daughter. Feli had asked her father to intervene because apparently the mother was "jealous" of her daughter's social life. "What did you do?", we asked. "I told her that she had to understand her mother". Once more we presented the image through the computer screen and corroborated that he was unwilling to even take a half an inch peek outside the cave. He did nothing. Not for his daughter nor for his wife. He was not interested, did not inquire, did not reflect, did not soil himself. Maximo began to sob covering his face with his great hands. We waited a little while. Then he asked looking at the sky, waiting for a celestial response. "What do I do? what do I do? God help

287

me, what do I do?".

We waited a little bit longer until he regained his composure, and we offered a proposal. Partly he took refuge in his character of fearful child and partly he was the adult we have in front of us, with the resources of an adult. He could make some movements to exit the cave ascertaining himself that no one was going to beat him up or reject or punish him. He could approach his daughter and ask her how she was doing. Perhaps offer her help or at least ask her if she needed anything he could provide. His face lit up. He knew his daughter wanted to move to a more comfortable house, and Maximo had the money needed. Did Feli ever asked you to help her? "No, never, she never asked for anything". We looked one more time at the image. The path had been drawn.

The wolf in sheep's clothes

Gimena was forty and she was married. She was the mother of two girls: Antonia, six and Francisca four. After working in the city of Buenos Aires for the Federal Police she had taken a sabbatical year. She was hoping to find a new direction in her life, and after reading some of my books, it seemed like an open door. This prompted her to consult with us. She looked frail, physically petite, very slim, with pale skin and clear eyes. She explained that she was preoccupied by an old conflict between her, her parents and siblings.

I want to point out that a detective is always on the job. During a century of military regimes, the Argentine Police Force has been institutionally involved in abuses against the citizenry; it has been an environment of repression, violence, corruption and authoritarianism. It does not mean that we will automatically assume that our client was directly affiliated with irregularities or abuses of power, but nevertheless, we had to keep this information in mind, which appeared incongruent with the ethereal and angelical image she portrayed at first sight. With these detective notes, we explained that we would start with her **human biography**.

She could not remember anything about her childhood and almost nothing about her adolescence. She claimed to have a very bad memory and only knew what she had been told. We explained how the mechanism of forgetting works and that usually the consciousness banishes to the shadow certain experiences, when the child would experience events that were too difficult or hostile for her age.

Her parents married when the father was eighteen and the mother was sixteen. We asked if the marriage was arranged because of a pregnancy, but Gimena did not know. For many years, the parents lived in the paternal grandparents' home. She was the oldest daughter, and she had a sister three years younger. She positively remembered the verbal and physical violence between her parents. In addition, her mother hated the paternal grandmother (with whom they lived). She described scenes that are not worth reproducing here, but in their aggregate, they painted an environment of family war. Gimena could not remember what was she doing during those times. She assured us that she was quiet and obedient, but in contrast, her sister would get into all kinds of trouble and get punished. For a long time, the family told a story about an episode where apparently, she had to take care of her sister, the sister fell, and she thought the sister had died and forever felt guilty because of this accident. The memories were so disorganized that it took us the first two meetings to organize them, to find a framework of truth and to leave other memories aside because they did not fit anything. In summary, we agreed that the violence in the home was frequent, especially the neglectfulness and lack of care for these girls.

Until now, we have a girl who is trying not to create more problems from those already present in the home. The over-adjustment -extremely common in many human biographies- is based on the children prioritizing the adults' needs to their own. This is called maternal abuse. She thought about it for a while and said that it was true that her mother would always say she would take great pains to care for the daughters, but she did not have any genuine recollection of receiving care from her mother.

Now it was necessary to approach her adolescence with at least two hypotheses: either she was going to continue repressing her basic needs by adapting herself to others, or she was going to establish bonds through fights, which was the system she was familiar with. We leaned toward the second option, but we needed to find out. We showed it like that, then with great assertion and defiant air, she affirmed that it was difficult to "defeat" her in any conflict. She showed us a scar on her waist, result of a knife wound where her sister wanted to stab her at age sixteen. But she left her sister with a worse scar on her face. However, she remembered that the sister got the worse punishments. This was the panorama.

She pursued her studies without difficulty, she had few friends except for one who has been her best friend until the present and is her oldest daughter's godmother. Gimena was considered the "quiet" one, while her sister was the "fierce" one, mouthy, confrontational, had many boyfriends and was "sharper" than Gimena, although she was the younger of the two. "Everybody thought that Silvina was the oldest, even physically she is a head taller than I".

Looking back at our notes it appeared that the incident with the knife did not fit with a quiet and even-tempered adolescent. We insisted on asking how she reacted when confronted with a conflict with her peers or when something she disliked happened. It was striking that she treasured so many examples. She remembered perfectly how she had pulled a lock of hair from a school mate after she had been mocked for her extreme slimness, or when she stuck another girl's head into the toilet to finish a fight. We responded that she was giving us the impression of a "snake in the grass". She was most fierce without anybody realizing it. She liked the idea.

The image of the "wolf in sheep's clothes" occurred to us. Precisely, she projected a very different image from what she was underhandedly capable. This she did not like as much. We greeted each other goodbye.

In the role of detectives, we had a problem: if our client's character is accustomed to lie, deceive, manipulate, and hide, she will do the same -without noticing it- within the investigation. Therefore, we need to increase the zoom of our lens to "catch" the smallest contradictions, because the deceit was part of her "well oiled" modality.

While constructing the **human biographies**, the challenge is to maintain on the same plane and simultaneously, the compassion for the child the client has been (with his survival mechanisms that allowed him to arrive here), and the alive and kicking adult thanks to those same mechanisms, that are often negative, hurtful and inflict suffering on others. In this case, it is easy to figure out: this girl found the solution to save herself by manipulating and deceiving (to hurt her sister in such a way that only the sister looked like the aggressor). If we think about it while observing this girl in a hostile environment, we can't but feel compassion.

Now, this individual grows, becomes an adult, and her infantile mechanisms continue to operate automatically, however, now we need to understand the little girl who lives inside her, and at the same time hold accountable the adult who is using this power to the detriment of everyone else. The professional's job is to observe both sides, childhood and adulthood in a synchronistic manner.

We welcomed her to the next meeting with these thoughts in mind, and we get her up to date on what we are starting to see. We talked about some important relationships she had with men during her youth, in which jealousy appears as the most interesting condiment. Deceits, betrayals, hysterias, unfaithfulness, in short, classic telenovelas that uncover the "manipulations" she introduced to come out victorious at each conflict. She related some anecdotes that are not worth detailing, but square perfectly with the "snake in the grass" image or the wolf in sheep's clothes. She would swipe out before her opponent would know what had happened, and she would end up eating the best morsel. Gimena would look at the image and would say: "Well, sometimes the devil comes out of me".

When she was twenty-two, through a connection from his father who was a captain in the police, she was offered an administrative position with the Federal Police. She advanced quickly climbing to higher positions to become Frontiers' Chief. We inquired about her job, but the answers did not fit. We had to clarify that we were not trying to obtain information as if we were "counter-police". We were not interested. We are not an organization of control from the State, or the FBI or anything similar. But for people who lie or distort the truth, they tend to find job systems that are in tune with their modality. Here, we are in front of a similar scenario: a secret territory, with power over others, directing information on the edge of legality, rubbing elbows with dubious business, bribery and corruption…We assured her that we did not need details, but it was understandable that she had found in the Police an environment of vertical authority, with permanent conflicts and abuses of power, very similar to what she had experienced in her home. "It is true -she answered-, in the Police, it's the law of the jungle, the strongest wins".

The wolf in sheep's clothes

We showed that Gimena had spent there eighteen comfortable years, as if she were in her own home.

In this institution, she met Octavio, her husband, who was a captain. He was single, twelve years her elder, lived by himself, had a car and, of course, a good amount of power. In the beginning she told us a tale of how Octavio was fascinated with her. We insisted with pointed questions until the story changed tune. I want to reiterate that looking at the image and assuming -in principle- that the deceit will be functioning automatically, the detectives cannot listen to a novel as if it were reality.

Inevitably we need to increase the lens through which we look. Finally, she revealed that Octavio wasn't single, but he was on the verge of separating from his wife; Gimena helped accelerate the process. He was the perfect candidate for her, especially because he handled a significant amount of power and a comfortable economic situation.

Shortly thereafter, Gimena was already living in her own flat. They had plans to start a family.

-What did Octavio want?

-What thing?

_To start a family.

_Mmmm, well, I don't know. He was working a lot.

-Then the plan to start a family was your goal, not something you shared.

-Well, I have never thought about it like this. It is true that I insisted very much, and I moved in almost without him realizing it.

-How were the first months of living together?

-With Octavio it was fine, the problem was his mother.

Well, of course, there were conflicts everywhere. Because it was the system that Gimena knew (and probably

Octavio also). She told us the details of the conflicts until she said: "I had to mark my territory". Sometimes, when we work with images, the clients will utter words served on a platter. We showed her the drawing and did not have to say another word. We were confirming the wolf was marking his territory. Of course, over many years, the constant fights, threats and promises left tracks on their relationship.

We asked many questions about Octavio, but we were surprised that the answers were vague. We could not figure out what Octavio desired, what was important to him, what did he ask for. We arrived at the conclusion that the wolf was only interested in satisfying herself but had no idea of what Octavio would have wanted to receive from her. Gimena was speechless. She had never thought about it. The stories of the fights did not make any sense either, as if the only motive was to keep a high level of adrenaline.

The pregnancies took a while to arrive, both worked a lot. In our role as detectives, we could imagine the birth of the first girl was going to be chaotic, because in this territory there was nothing soft to receive her, no quietude, calm or wellbeing. Gimena discharged a torrent of complaints: she was unable to breastfeed, that it hurt, the pediatrician told her that her milk was no good, that mother-in-law was interfering, Octavio did not help her, the baby rejected her, she had been an omnipresent mother. Good grief! Gimena, let us look at your scenario with eyes wide open. There cannot be an omnipresent mother in favor of a child when she is on the alert to defend herself from all her imaginary adversaries.

-When did you return to work?

-Forty-five days later I ran out of maternity leave.

-It was a relief, right?

-How do you know?

I want you to know that logic speaks for itself. We are not judging whether Gimena was or wasn't a good mother. This is not the issue. The only matter is that the wolf had its goals and was not thinking about anything else but to achieve them. The best way was that no one noticed that behind this tiny and pale woman there was a ferocious predator.

It was very difficult to approach Antonia's life from the point of view of the baby she had been. Gimena denied, twisted or simply invented. Antonia went to a nursery from the time she was forty-five days old and when she was three years old, she attended a full-time childcare center. Of course, the girl cried a lot, but according to Gimena, "later she would calm down". We told her that we would not admit those lies and that she could stop lying to herself. It was not necessary. We had to "unpack" almost everything she talked about Antonia's first years. We imagined and told Gimena real scenes and she would finally admit them, one by one. This is the professional's required job, because the scenes that we "tell ourselves", we later "water" them and make them "grow" in our imaginations and expand our deceived discourses to leave us satisfied as adults. And the children adrift.

Later we discussed Francisca' pregnancy and birth; the family's rhythm hasn't changed. There was no breastfeeding either, nor patience; this child was sent to daycare very early, she got sick a lot and this was all Gimena could rescue from her daughters' lives.

At the next meeting Gimena arrived with a shaken countenance. She had cried a lot thinking about those years with her daughters. She had realized that she would keep her adrenaline through the roof, busy in her fights with

Octavio and without connecting with her daughters. She also confessed that Octavio used to tell her: "No one else knows how screwed up you are".

Finally, Gimena wanted to relate about a great fight she was having with her parents and siblings. We interrupted her, we told her that we could listen for a few minutes, but the important thing was that she recognized that without the fight's adrenaline, she was left without identity. And before entering a discussion about who is right and who is just or unjust, it was incumbent on her to understand how those fights had nourished her throughout her life. We needed to observe the entire field, since the details of each fight were not important. Gimena lost heart, as if we had removed the fire that kept her alive.

The family's conflict revolved around a certain amount of money they had asked as a loan and had not been repaid. End of the story. Gimena insisted on telling us the details and to complain about her parents, but we did not allow her. Why? Because in doing so she would have "introduced us into her field" to look at her scenario from her trench. We would lose objectivity. I insist that it is important not to listen. Not to listen to anything at all to complaints, because we lose the focus of what is primordial within the game in the global scenario. The striking part about this story of the loan is that Gimena had gained economically the most! Although she was telling a story of how unjust her parents had been. This is the advantage of being a wolf in sheep's clothes: we are used to manipulate and change the vision of reality to confuse the adversary. On the other hand, the more energy she invested in her fury or the injustice regarding her parents' decisions, her daughters received less protection. We looked at two little girls in the middle of this mess.

This was the sketch of this accompaniment. To support her so that she could access emotional resources to protect her daughters. Put down her arms. Take off her costume from time to time. Try to be sincere. Tolerate what others may tell her. Accept the truth. Attempt some humility. Connect with her fear. Listen, contemplate, and if possible, agree to some of her daughters' requests. It was a two-year process, with one step forward and three steps back, each time. Frustrating. Tedious. At times feeling that Gimena would come charging up again with organized lies. Other times, lifting the veil. And others with sharp weapons. However, we had drafted the path and had a clear objective, and if Gimena was willing, we were available to accompany her with a firm step.

The closed little package

Julieta was twenty-eight years old; she did not have a partner or children. She was a graphic designer. She had read some of my books and wanted to consult out of curiosity since one of her friends had experienced her own **human biography** investigative process. She was an attractive, likeable and communicative young woman.

Her mother was a sociologist. Since she was fourteen, Julieta had experienced multiple therapies. She said that her "self-esteem was very low". We asked her who had said "such thing". She was surprised but assured us this is the issue that always cropped up in all her therapies. We responded that we would not take any interpretation as true, but at most they were mere interpretations. In time, we would find out together. We began her **human biography.**

Her mother came from an intellectual middle-class family. Her maternal grandfather had been a renowned historian and writer who died when Julieta was six years old, although still retained the myth he had earned in his lifetime. The maternal grandmother, who was still alive, and the maternal aunts and uncles mingled in sophisticated, artistic and intellectual circles. The mother started dating the father at age twenty-one, when they were Sociology students. The father was from a similar family of high-middle-class extract, not as intellectual but closer to the entrepreneurial environment. The father was "the handsome one", the women's prized candidate at the club they attended.

Two girls were born from this young marriage between

mom and dad, Isabel and Julieta with five years difference between them. Julieta remembered that she fought a lot with her sister but could not explain why. She could only remember that she did not tolerate her. It was said that Isabel was dad's favorite, and she was mom's favorite.

This subject of "favorites" within families tends to be very confusing. First of all….no adult really chooses anyone. If the children were "chosen" they would be filled with love by someone. This rarely occurs. Julieta had very few memories from childhood, and to each question she responded with memories about what mom liked, what mom did, or what preoccupied mom. Julieta considered that she had a happy childhood. We asked at length. Although it was not a childhood of terrible emotional abandonment as we are accustomed to identifying, the adults' true awareness of the girl's needs, was absent.

At age three, she began attending a daycare center. She did not like going there, she remembered that she would wet herself, but the mother would patiently change her clothes and send her anyway. Her mother was delicate, would talk to her gently, however Julieta was never able to convey her fears and her desire to stay at home. She had very few memories from her early childhood: only her shyness, the fights with her sister and mother's enchanting world. Not much more. We asked many questions, but Julieta would answer with laughter as if she were a ten-year-old instead of an adult wanting to inquire into her own self.

Although the mother had an intense social life, apparently, she left the girls cooped up in the house much of the time. During her adolescence they only had permission to go to the social club they belonged to or visit a few close friends. If the mother did not know the family well, they would not get permission to go out. In any event,

Julieta enjoyed staying home to play. She told with nostalgia that her house was partly a "museum"; they preserved awards, photos and tributes from her grandfather, which Julieta showed off with pride when her friends came to visit.

We looked for additional memories from her childhood. There were no fights between the parents, no discussions or conflicts. Her parents separated when Julieta was nine, but she does not remember anything specific. We investigated a bit more and only appeared silence in the house, as the most salient element. Mom coordinated several study and research groups that met in the front part of the house; therefore, it was necessary to stay silent not to bother.

Julieta's memories about happiness are related to the comfortable life, the pleasant neighborhood, the high quality of her school and the nicely appointed home. The comfort of daily life was sufficient. Compared with other life stories, there was nothing horrific, although she was far from having a loving and warm childhood that every child deserves. Julieta was understanding perfectly, and later she added that during her adolescence she became a "rebel".

Before we continue, we observe the panorama. There were few options for her to rebel so much, especially because the environment was so comfortable. But we had to find out.

When she arrived at her adolescence, she had more awareness about her parents' separation. She had a shallow life: school, club and outings. Her parents did not argue among themselves, but soon there was dad's new girlfriend and mom's new boyfriend, and both parents took the girls as hostages. I will spare you the details: on broad strokes these two adolescents resolved the issue by leaving the house and finding refuge in entertainment and outings with friends. The easier option was to flood themselves with shallowness and this is what Julieta did. Outings, dancing clubs, expensive clothes, makeup and general fashion consumption.

During her adolescence, the lack of parental gaze became more evident. She self-regulated by moving within a reduced group of girlfriends, since both her mother and father were behaving as adolescents themselves, busy with their own courtships and had little contact with their daughters' emotional reality. During this period Julieta and her sister became even more distanced.

Coincidentally, Julieta's mother began to complain about her "rebelliousness". What was Julieta doing? She would be upset at trivialities. Also, because she was aware of her attractiveness, she thought about becoming a fashion model. Her mother discouraged her on pursuing this endeavor. Nothing more. We looked for real "rebelliousness", but other than being a bit upset at home, we could not find any situation that would indicate the abandonment of the family's modality.

In summary, she was enclosed in a miniscule environment, always in the same school with the same girlfriends. We look for specific interests, hopes, personal desires…, but -once the fantasy of becoming a fashion model was disallowed- there was nothing else.

When she finished high school, she did not know what to study. Her only activity was to go out dancing with her friends. She did not have boyfriends. She took a short modelling course, learned to apply makeup and to dress better. She never applied to any modelling jobs. We asked if she talked about it with her mother again. No. She had discarded the option herself; besides she had taken the course for her own "enjoyment". There she had a short relationship with the hairdresser with whom there was no sexual encounter. We pointed out, that although there were no great damages throughout her young life, the emotional distance and the comfortable and enclosed environment left her with a hurtful shallowness. We had the feeling of being in front of a girl, prisoner in a small world, having explored hardly anything outside her immediate environment. We thought of showing her the image of a pretty little package wrapped with ribbon.

It was obvious that inside she was going to find all the safety and comfort she needed. But she remained prisoner of a fenced-in world. It was not good or bad, however she would likely reject at first sight any access to new knowledge and even a comprehensive self-understanding.

During her last year of graphic design school, Julieta met a young man who was attending a class with her. Luis tried to seduce her. He was a coarser young man, from a less wealthy family, who was working at a bookstore to help pay for his studies. But Julieta was afraid. Obviously, anything coming from outside her package -meaning, her tiny known universe- would be dangerous.

The school year ended, but Luis continued communicating with her and inviting her to go out. Julieta consulted with her girlfriends, who firmly advised her against it. Who knew him? Where did he "come from"? It is true that they did not run in the same circles. We did not have any opinion about it, but we proposed that she look at the closed little package and the logic of the scenario.

It came to pass that one-day Luis showed up at her home. Finally, she accepted to go out with him, and Julieta had her first sexual experiences that weren't very satisfying. She had not even told him that she was a virgin. Why? "I

305

was afraid he would make fun of me". The whole picture was coherent with her lack of experience and seclusion. She did not want any of her friends and much less her family to find out about this relationship. Why? "Because he did not seem to be a young man from high society". It was obvious that the shallowness, the appearances, and the external gaze supported the minimal universe in which Julieta moved.

It was striking that this young man was delicate, cared and was genuinely interested in her. However, he came from a world "outside the package". This is what we had to observe together. It wouldn't be of any help to figure out if this young man was good or bad, if he was worthy or not, if she had to "clear" him with her girlfriends or had to leave him; instead we had to figure out in which corner of the scenario he was located. It was clear that this woman-girl was not ready to have sex or support a loving relationship. She accepted. She was an intelligent young woman; however, she was shut away inside a crystal bubble.

This brief relationship had taken place a year before the consultation. It was high time for her to stand on her feet and review the advantages of living inside the package with its economic benefits, belonging to a social circle and the shallowness. The benefits were obvious.

It is possible that destiny would propose to overcome this comfort, therefore, her challenge was to be alert and not forego future opportunities for growth. Our work was done. We met a few times more. We could propose if she was interested in taking apart the beautiful package with ribbon and bow and come out into the world, or not. Perhaps the moment had yet to arrive. It was positive to know that at some point, the door was going to open.

The little closed package

The petulant child

Gabriel was a pleasant man of thirty-nine. He entered the consultation room with a frown, distrustful and measuring each word he said. He had two sons, Teo, was five and Valentino, was eight months old. He was "sent" by his wife, who was a fan of my books. He was a director at a textile company. His wife had worked with him but was now dedicating herself to the children. There was nothing that concerned him now except that he could not find his "place" as a father in front of his children. We offered to begin the work.

His mother had been a schoolteacher all her professional life, until she retired. His father grew up in the countryside, and later became a public servant until he passed away when Gabriel was twenty-six. Gabriel was the second child; two sons and two daughters. Mom had named him the "good" and "quiet" one. There were very few childhood memories. He played with the neighborhood children, he was timid, but had some good friends who would take the initiative to call him to come out to play.

His parents always lived together, spoke little among themselves, except for the subjects related to daily life. The father "had a life" outside the home and when he would return at night, he complained that the mother "did not talk". It is true, the mother did not talk. She was not moody, she simply closed herself in her shell and did not share anything. Neither happiness, sadness nor upsets. Absolutely nothing. The children were used to this. They did not ask or share anything important with their mother. Gabriel enjoyed best to go outside to play with his friends. We inquired further into the relationship with the mother; no tender memories appeared. Nor of violence. We told him that it must have been very hard for a child -the epitome of vitality and movement- to adapt to the quiet and silence. Gabriel was moved, he had never thought about it before.

We explored more about his father, since he was a man searching for something more vital outside the house, but he responded that the relationship between them was sour. There was an episode the mother had related many times (therefore Gabriel was unsure whether this was his own memory or a "reconstruction at a later time"), in which the mother had left the house and, since he cried much, the father hit him and named him "petulant". We told him that beyond the father's lack of skills, his mother had left him in the hands of a man incapable of taking care of him, and later she endeavored on repeating over and over again that he was petulant, when she herself was unable to organize a bond of solidarity and affection.

The father had many personal interests: he participated in an orchestra, had friends and an intense social life outside his work. Instead, the mother lived only between the school where she worked and the house. We asked if Gabriel joined his father in his outings, but he rejected this idea emphatically. We showed him that this rejection must originate in a strong maternal discourse, otherwise it had no logic. Any child will accept accompanying the adults that go out of the house, to fun celebrations or have relationships with other people. He had never thought about it, but yes, it appeared coherent. Until this moment we have a quiet, silent child who seems functional to the mother. He behaved according to what mom needed, without contradicting or demanding anything from her. We need to imagine how he was going to confront adolescence, coming from a childhood so demure and obedient to the maternal needs.

The shyness and obedience never facilitate the transit along adolescence, which requires a modicum of anger, strength, and courage. In fact, his adolescence was complex. To top it off, he did not like soccer, which for young men in a country like Argentina, it would create difficulties in the field of friendships. He was an average student. Since he was handsome, quiet and well-mannered, he was able to have a few girlfriends. He remembered he was upset with his father, but as much as we inquired, we could not find a significant episode, and we concluded that he was simply in sync with mom's upset.

Since the family lived a neighborhood in the periphery, when he finished high school, he moved closer to the town center, at the home of some uncles. He needed to free himself from the home's tensions and this geographical change was very significant. He looked for a short course of studies related with marketing and two years later he was working in small businesses until he obtained a position at a larger firm. He was able to adapt to the rhythm of the big city right away.

Soon after his father was diagnosed with cancer. At this moment, he perceived something that left him perplexed: the mother dedicated herself with love and selflessness to care for her husband. Didn't the mother spent all her life incredibly upset at the father? He laughed, accepting that he had always asked the same question. After all, Gabriel had squandered his energy to defend his mother's "position" by unconsciously confronting his father…assuming this is how he would obtain his mother's acceptance, in vain.

It was true. Now he could see it clearly. In fact, his three siblings had always had a good relationship with the father. Sometimes we are so restricted by our roles that we lose perspective. His father died a few months later, however he could not let go of his upset even after death. We greeted him at the end of the consultation telling him that we saw a man who has difficulty "stepping outside" of his established opinions, with few words -like his mother-something "closed", fixed, obstinate. At the next meetings we would attempt to draw a sketch of his scenario and his survival character.

At age thirty he met Liza, his wife. It had been difficult to conquer her, because he would not dare talk to her. She fascinated him but he could not find the words to express to her his feelings. This was the apparent reason why other girlfriends had left him. He had a hard time talking and expressing his feelings. On the other hand, when things did not go as he expected, he would enter the "upset zone" from which he could not get out.

This assertion seemed very interesting to us. In fact, it was difficult to obtain information from Gabriel; his answers were limited, as if he were measuring each word. In addition, we had the feeling that if we had made a mistake in any assessment, he would get very mad. It was nothing concrete, barely a perception that was floating in the air. What is this of entering in the "upset zones"? According to Gabriel, he felt that the other "had to guess" what he wanted. Otherwise, he would feel betrayed. This was his wife's primary complaint.

We talked for a while about our childhood deficiencies. There is a period as babies and young children, when our mother should "guess" or at least "decipher" what happens to us to be able to satisfy us. However, this happens so rarely, that the children learn that "it isn't even worth asking" because we already know anyway that "mom won't understand". According to Gabriel's account, it appeared that he got stuck in that period waiting for "someone to guess". If this did not happen…he would "close up".

Then we showed him the image of a closed child, petulant, with arms crossed, upset and waiting for someone to ask him for forgiveness.

Gabriel thought it was funny and started laughing. He said: "If my wife sees this, she would be rubbing her hands". Then he became more serious and said this was it. Then, on the edge of tears, he said he did not remember a single happy birthday celebration when he was a child, and he did not like the gifts his parents bought him. Obviously, there weren't any adults capable of "guessing" what he liked, to be attentive, to ask him and take him into consideration. This happened in the past. Then he let go of a long-withheld sob. "I don't know how to overcome all this; everything makes me mad". We waited for a long while so he could cry out all that was inside.

It was important to differentiate the child who cannot ask because the adult was not going to listen, from the adult who has resources and decides not to use them. Perhaps because he had cemented and "created his identity" there. Or perhaps because he obtained benefits. We had to find out.

Gabriel and Liza dated for a few years before they moved together. They had been colleagues at work, and they got along in the professional environment. Liza had always asked Gabriel to speak up, explain and express himself. She had somewhat learned to guess his requests or emotions. Other times, even if she did perceive them, she did not put much effort to satisfy him automatically, especially since the birth of the first child.

During the next meeting, already with the image in hand, we tackled the birth of the children and the beginning of family life. What can we assume in our role of detectives? If Gabriel was still functioning as a petulant child who required to be "satisfied" by guessing…he was going to compete for attention with his children, who being very young, they absolutely needed the mother to interpret their every need. We told him so.

Then he remembered a recent episode, when he was shopping at the market, the older child asked him why he never purchased "sweets" for him. Gabriel responded automatically: "Because you never told me that you liked them". He understood that now in his role of adult, it was his turn to "perceive" what his children desired. It was a great insight.

We investigated in detail many aspects of family life, and after a few meetings we found a subject that was worthwhile approaching. Gabriel thought it was "unfair" that Liza decided to take a year off from work without pay, to dedicate herself entirely to the children, especially the newborn. Why was he the only one having to work? This was a disconcerting comment. Or not so much if we directed our gaze at the image of a child throwing a tantrum. We told him so. This looked more like a tantrum than the thought of a mature man, the father of two children and husband of a mature woman.

Then he continued complaining about the justice and injustice between the genders, that in the Scandinavian countries the fathers also have paternity benefits, etcetera. We dedicated ourselves to listen for a while and to observe him during a "fit".

The petulant child

At the end we asked him if he wanted a lollipop. There he "returned" to reality. We waited until after he had drained his fury and asked him how he was doing at work, how were his money issues. These questions allowed us to conclude that he had a number of complex situations at work, and he felt too alone to confront them. Very well. Why were we obligated to "guess" that "this" is what was happening to him?

We asked if the family needed Liza's salary. No. We asked if Liza would be happier going back to work or staying home with the children, when they are so little, especially the second one. We asked if he had discussed this with his wife. No. The advantages of not talking were evident. It was a way to enclose himself in his known character of petulant child. We made it clear that our detective work was going to be concentrated in reviewing how he was trying to compete with his wife's assumed "advantages", including those of his children. To close himself up, to get upset, and become obstinate have until now brought him some benefits, but if he continued, his children were going to pay the consequences. It was time to grow up.

Transcendence

We could relate thousands upon thousands of stories about people's **human biographies**, and even then, it would be difficult to encompass the magnitude of personal experiences, feelings, contradictions, and ambivalences; in addition to looking at the intimacy that is established between the human biographer and the client. It is an enormous challenge, on behalf of one and the other. The clients must be ready to walk to the limits of our own abyss, while the HBrs are confronted by the client s' natural distrust and their demands for solutions. Then, it is best to listen with detective's ears, and place our intuitive capabilities at the service of the truth, remembering that we will always search for a global application, including a more spiritual one. Greater than any of us.

Each time that we approach with respect and sincerity, the internal wound of a human being, we are initiating a path we do not know where it will lead us to. We do not have objectives, expect results, nor issue judgements, and of course, we do not offer advice. Here is the proposal: let us walk together. As we enter further into most life stories, we acquire more training, and we refine our perceptions. In any event, there are no guaranties.

Beyond the fact that some readers may have identified more with one story than another (or perhaps they did not identify with any), I confess that, once we have attended to a several hundreds of individuals, we conclude that life stories tend to be similar. Why? Because -within our system of civilization- when we were children, we did not receive the basic necessary emotional safety. Everything that happens later will be a permanent search of compensation for that hostility we experienced during our childhood.

The organization of the **human biography** I propose is only the first step. I want to believe that in one or two generations we will be doing something else. The human biography attempts to lay a blanket of truth over reality. When I say it like this, it looks obvious, but I have already explained that in people's everyday lives, there is a vast distance separating our internal realities (past or present, it doesn't matter) and what we believe or interpret about those realities. Here is the entire issue.

It could take our entire life to undertake this path. To understand our entire scenario, the true role played by each person who has been essential in our life, to relate our childhood with our youth and adulthood, to recognize the character that allowed us to survive, to daily observe this character react automatically, to attempt to change some aspects of this character, to live with more agreements every day and to love our neighbor -even when we know we have not been sufficiently loved when we were children- appear to be impractical tasks. However, all this continues to be the first step. Perhaps our descendants will follow in this wake: our children, nephews and nieces, apprentices or godchildren. The intention is to train in this way of looking at ourselves not only for our own benefit, but for the benefit of those who will live in the future.

Moreover, all personal inquiry -courageous and honest- will inevitably bring us closer to Our Higher Self, that is, that part of ourselves that yearns to transcend while searching for truth, attempting to understand what service we have been invited to unfold for the benefit of our fellow humans. The issue is that to reach Our Higher Self, it is necessary to strip ourselves off the masks and confront what is, in the here and now.

We are not guaranteed a state of joy and happiness by contacting Our Higher Self. We have seen how, we have learned since we were children to live disguised under a character not to make our parents mad or to respond to their expectations. This is a mechanism we have honed since the day we were born. It is interesting to observe those who accompany these processes of encountering our own shadow sometimes "give permission" to another adult to allow herself the right to live internally as it is appropriate instead of continuing to respond to mom or dad's unconscious desires. In any event, to lay bare our internal truth, is a good beginning in our path to accepting ourselves. Only then we will travel from self-realization to transcendence.

All this looks very pretty, but it requires much work and dedication. It is also important that we can recognize when "spirituality" functions as an infantile refuge, instead of being the consequence of having previously been in contact with our True Self. In any case, we must "touch" our shadow, the emotional abandonment, the pain for all that we have not received or the hope that mom would love us how we would have needed to be loved. From my point of view, it is necessary to transit along the dark aspects of our identity, taken by the hand by an experienced, generous, open, wise and contemplative person. The construction of the **human biography** is a possible path. It is not the only one or the best. It is one among many modalities. All these systems of inquiry are akin to a "road map" that human beings have developed, to guide us in the processes of self-knowledge. Once we have approached our personal history and our family plot, the role we have occupied within our scenario, the benefits we derived from our characters and the binding games, then, in full awareness and understanding of our emotional reality, perhaps we will be able to transcend and be at the service of humanity.

Who can fulfill the conditions to train in this endeavor of accompanying others in the construction of their **human biography**? Whoever wants to. First, we must be able and willing to confront our own demons. It is not necessary to have a perfect, and happy life devoid of conflicts. I have never met anyone who can resemble this. But it is inevitable that we know the pain of darkness and that we train our gaze to observe the global realities with an open and generous gaze in favor of everyone's evolution.

Only then we will truly understand that advice is useless, that we do not know more than anyone else, but we have simply been accustomed to look at reality from the shadow. The light does not blind us. Nor the light of the pretty speeches or the light of the overwhelming or charming personalities, or the light of the identifications. To accompany another to know himself is to take him by the hand into his own darkness. I don't know of anything else this loving that one human being can do for another.

I admit this is an ungrateful task. We tend to fusion with all the suffering and all the hopes. It can also happen that we have no patience for all the purely social activities, especially when they are false, when the bonds happen between character and character. These masks that have been useful for such a long time to protects us, fall into disuse and hurt us. According to the social "mores", we behave politely doing what our character knows how to do. The known is always safe for an infantile or a very wounded soul. However, it comes a time when we can no longer fail to see what we are able to see. We perceive the naked soul, we see the fear, the many men and women needing to be loved, transiting though life stuck in our past wounds. To know it, to confirm it, to understand it, to know our emotional reality -however much suffering or lack we have experienced- is the first step toward transcendence.

From the individual to the collective

Mi earlier books were focused on the detailed description of the maternal world and the difficulty we have as mothers in loving our children within a solidary system, that is, prioritizing the child's comfort. I have explained in every one of my books, in different approaches, when as adults we have difficulty in providing what the child is asking for, it is fitting to review our degree of childhood emotional abandonment instead of casting blame on the creature. The assumption is simple: if during our childhood we were emotionally hungry, this experience continues to live in our interior. Then, when we become adults and it is our turn to nourish another -in this case the child-, we will not have anything to give. This is when the demand seems "disproportionate". How do we resolve this? Usually, we adopt a variety of theories -unfortunately sponsored by debatable "psychologisms"- to support our point of view that "we are right" and the child is wrong and "needs limits". It is the other's fault.

If during our childhood suffered emotional abandonment in addition to violence, abuse, sexual repression or maternal imbalances that have undermined our capacity to love, obviously those emotional resources will be lacking when the time comes to love another, adult or child. Unfortunately, our "lifestyle", the education we received, the emotional distance we experienced growing up, the assumed "normality" and all the resources at the hands of the patriarchy, have pierced us without our awareness. I have written and published a dozen books on this subject.

I have later organized a system and written a possible methodology to help everyone access his own shadowy material. That is, to understand why we are unable to love as much as we want. All these books are an invitation to reflect, as they do not offer general opinions, but proposals for personal inquiry. All this has been written; it is published. Many of my articles, conferences and videos circulate in the virtual universe. However, the shadow is stronger. The collective unconscious calms down only when it can position my name related to a thought where I am "in favor of" something about a certain subject, and "against" something else. It shows contempt by considering that only mothers are interested in "this thing about maternity".

I always considered that "this thing about maternity" concerns us all, since we have all been born from the womb of a mother, and what happened to us in connection with our mother or the person who fulfilled the maternal role, determined the evolution of our lives. Especially if we are unwilling to inquire about what happened to us or what we did with what happened to us; to be free to make decisions about what we want to continue doing based on what happened to us.

I have described in other books that the emotional abandonment, the violence and the domination of the adults' desires above the children's desires is intrinsic and semantic of the patriarchy, that is, it is built-in into our civilization. It is rare to find children to whom "this" has not happened. Since our earliest childhood, we have been trained in the domination system, because we have been raised subdued to the other's desire. Later, out automatic impulse will be placed between these two options: living dominated or have a slice of power to dominate others to the extent we can. At this point, the first possible individual action is available to us: to inquire about who we are, what happened to us and then detect if we can change anything to the benefit of others, or if this is too complicated. We have much work to do in the individual and family environments.

The collective life reflects on a larger scale the individual lives

Thus far, we are clear that we have learned the domination mechanisms since our early childhood. These modalities are then multiplied inside the heart of families, villages, cities, and of course, the organization of countries. It is only a matter of magnitude. Whatever people do in our private lives, it also operates in the collective bonds. Our patterns of relating within an individual format are equivalent to the functioning at a social scale. It is the same thing, at a larger magnitude. In fact, the collective life is always a reflection of the sum of the individual lives.

All communities create an idea for a possible order to manage the collective life. We vote into office whomever we vote, whether we are democrats, republicans, socialists, liberals or communists…, we will do whatever we can do as individuals. Exactly because we are the people we are (emotionally abandoned and hungry children; I am sorry to be so repetitive on this point), we establish domination systems whereby some individuals will obtain more power to the detriment of others, who will remain subjugated to the weakness and abuse. Nothing else is possible because this is the only modality bond we know. In addition, we are totally unaware of this.

People do in public life as they do in their private life. Whether we are a public servant or a merchant; a teacher or farmer; a homemaker going to a political demonstration or a businessperson; a student or a tourist. The way we establish social bonds, work, study, travel, walk along the street, or comply with our duties belong to the public arena. If we have adopted the character of the explosive individual, we will be explosive in all aspects of our public life. If we are a fearful individual, abused, lost in himself, this is how we will function in society. If we manipulate information, we deal in half-truths, whether we work, teach, or manage an enterprise.

By observing the individual cases I have described in this book, you have verified how complex it is for a person to recognize his own emotional reality. Then, once he gets in touch with the level of abuse, deceit, violence, and distance from herself, it is very difficult to change. The commitment with oneself and the intention to get in touch with the soul of the child we have been is intricate and painful. Imagine how difficult it would be for millions of people to be willing to go through these processes with this level of honesty.

On the private level, we have seen that to inquire onto the maternal (or the person who raised us) discourse is exceedingly complex. At the beginning, we blindly believe what mom told us. This is truly what happened when we were children. All children believe our mother or the person who cared for us or protected us. Later when we grow up and we not only continue to believe what mom told us, but we will also believe anything that resembles the infantile comfort. The discourse needs to simply include "something" that takes us back to a sweet sensation of the past. To the extent that each of us has organized his own "deceived discourse" within a group of ideas, judgements, and comfortable opinions, we will not need to reflect or think something "different" (than the group). We are already moving onto the collective plane. Indeed, since we are all navigating together in the same direction, people will take as "certain" any opinion proffered with sufficient emphasis.

Politics

This is how the speeches of men and women politicians or holders of power, are written. Why is it so frequent that unbalanced individuals, often ignorant, arrive at unthinkable levels of power? Because the common folk constitute an enormous mass of people who are submissive to the desires of others, since this mirrors our childhood experience.

He who embodies a consolidated desire, will subjugate us. What is it that dominates us? The fascination for this aroma of a well-known situation. There is something like mom, like dad or the worse predator of our childhood -whom we have loved- who tells us he will protect us. That peace times are coming. That we will be a fantastic nation. That we will defend our rights with our teeth and nails. That from his hand will come forth progress or we will be saved. However, for "this" to happen, we need to obey them. Support them. Vote for them. Love them. Admire them. Be attentive to what happens "to them" and to their needs. In this game of glances, we have disappeared as individuals.

Does it remind you of anything? Yes, it places us back in the same dynamic of attention and gaze that mom demanded. If something did not go well, it was because, we, children, did not behave as she expected. On the other hand, life would travel along the adults' mishaps. The children were not allowed in the game. Therefore, we had to observe the adults. In fact, today, we still remember all our parents' preoccupations and sufferings, but we do not remember our own. This is the key to recognizing where our energy is diverted and how our desires or infantile needs disappeared from the family's scenario. The same logic works on the collective scale. Our personal interests disappear when we give priority to the interests of those who dominate us.

Since communication has become globalized and the electronic media have become as necessary as the air we breathe, what the communication media generates every moment has become a toxic nourishment for our thoughts, our energy, our good humor and our creativity. Just like in the past we were waiting on mom or dad's humor, now we are in thrall of the humor of Tokyo's stock market, when we are a geography professor, an employee at a shoe store, a fine arts' student, or a retired school headmaster. A total nonsense. This is yet another corner where we can observe in intellectual terms the reaches of domination.

Within the heartbeat of domination, individuals become "preoccupied" with the subjects those who dominate us wants us occupied. "Communication" is a very powerful tool. We can draw a parallel with the "maternal discourse", the "discourse of the deceived self" and the discourse of the "deceived collective". They all respond to the same dynamics at a different scale. In either case, we are "distant" from our own selves. We do not know what happens to us, what we want or where we are going.

Continuing along this thought, we will admit that it is easy to believe just anything: that this one politician is better, foundational, the only one who will help us grow as a nation, progressive, advanced or what have you. As children who have suffered abuse, we need to project an imagined care toward us on behalf of those who "decide" at the government level. Then, any advertisement, emphatic speech or threat will trap us by touching our most infantile weak spot. The place of fear. If many of us are afraid, the fear increases. In addition, what the "majority" thinks is taken as the "truth" in the highway of conventional ideas.

The most efficient way to "figure out" that we are inside a "collective deceit" is to first inquire about the individual "deceived discourses". It occurs to me that to unravel the global deceit will only be possible when a handful of millions of people can undertake this adventure.

Just like an adult can easily abuse a child, or a powerful person a weaker one, in the same manner it is easy to dominate entire countries. Once more, this is a matter of scale. We design this system since birth, by imposing it onto each newborn. The desire for unbridled power is understandable: it is sweet revenge. At the end what is the power of a few over many? The result of an imperative need not to be hurt. If we had been raised within a loving system, we would use our personal power for the benefit of others and we would not need it to soothe our fears to the extent that others nourish us or are afraid of us. These are the two sides of the same coin. Dominator and dominated we come from the same place of heartbreak and emotional abandonment. We will only be able to take apart those toxic dynamics if we recognize the infantile fear that devours us.

If we do not remove our masks, we will continue to eat the garbage we are fed, consuming the blogs, podcasts and TV programs, paying to see toxic films, going to the plaza to cheer the candidate of the day, sending our children to authoritarian schools, ingesting contaminating medications, breathing poisoned air, working at jobs we have not chosen, fighting to exhaustion for something we ignore and defending obsolete ideas.

Likely, the most terrifying fact is to become aware that we don't even have our own principles. Once we begin a courageous investigation of our shadow aspects and we tackle the painful reality of our childhood experiences, we won't have any choice but to review the entirety of our preconceived ideas, our "likes", our definitions, our opinions, and our beliefs: that every social, political or economic "fight" is a gigantic misunderstanding.

To love your fellow human being

Is there anything to be changed in the public arena, or in the political environment? Possibly yes, if we include the personal changes, and we recover our capacity to **love our fellow human being**. The "fellow" is someone very close to us. It is our pet. Our brother. Our office mates. Our child. It is our ex-mother-in-law. Do we need to get along with everybody? No. It would be silly to pretend this. However, we can strive to understand and have compassion for the child we have been. Then we will be able to understand and have compassion even toward those who hurt us, to those who today do not care for us, who mistreat us without being aware.

Change won't be possible unless we individually assume the responsibility of understanding ourselves and our fellow human. There has never been a political movement or governmental regime that has ever demonstrated that solidarity between humans can be systematically established at a collective level. There is no possible political change if we continue to believe that it is a matter of fighting our adversaries. This has nothing to do with a possible loving order. The political fights and the "struggles" are not helpful to anyone, except to those who need to nourish themselves from a specific battle or who hope to gain more power.

It is incumbent upon all of us to contribute a grain of sand in favor of a more caring and ecological, more solidary and egalitarian, more spiritually, intellectually and creatively elevated society. To this end we need to understand that personal fights are only survival resources from the past, and they do no longer have a reason to exist, if we understand them within the context of our experience of emotional abandonment.

I am convinced that the historical revolutions brew and grow withing each loving relationship. Between a man and a woman; between an adult and a child; between two men or between five women; in a friends' circle; in the center of solidary families.

It is time to mature. Today we have the duty to offer our abilities, our emotional intelligence and our generosity to the world, which is so needed. The **human biography** as a system of personal inquiry, it is my personal contribution so that it can become a reality.

Index

Printed in Great Britain
by Amazon

26009656R00185